How many men does it take
to screw in a lightbulb? . . .
<u>None!</u>

THE MODERN WOMAN'S GUIDE TO HOME REPAIR

The Modern Woman's Guide to HOME REPAIR

Jeni E. Munn
and Joan Sittenfield

A Perigee Book

A Perigee Book
Published by The Berkley Publishing Group
A member of Penguin Putnam Inc.
200 Madison Avenue
New York, NY 10016

Copyright © 1997 by Jeni E. Munn and Joan Sittenfield
Book design by Irving Perkins Associates
Cover design by Charles Björklund
Cover illustration by Liz Conrad
Illustrations by Boni Grossman-Smith and Alexander Comas
Cartoons by Wende Bibo
Hair and makeup for back cover photograph of Jeni Munn by Lesli Berlin
Photograph of Jeni E. Munn by James Kelly
Photograph of Joan Sittenfield by Harry Langdon

First edition: September 1997

Published simultaneously in Canada.

The Putnam Berkley World Wide Web site address is http://www.berkley. com

Library of Congress Cataloging-in-Publication Data

Sittenfield, Joan D.
    The modern woman's guide to home repair / Joan D. Sittenfield and
Jeni E. Munn. — 1st ed.
      p. cm.
    ISBN 0-399-52336-7
    1. Dwellings—Maintenance and repair—Amateurs' manuals.
I. Munn, Jeni E. II. Title.
TH4817.3.S57 1997
643'.7—DC21

                    96-54027
                    CIP

Printed in the United States of America

10 9 8 7 6 5 4 3 2 1

This book is dedicated to every woman who has ever had the urge to pick up a hammer and the men who inspired them to do so.

Also, Jeni Munn would like to thank her mother, Norma Munn, for her love and encouragement throughout the years.

Joan Sittenfield dedicates this to her therapist . . . just because.

Contents

Acknowledgments ix

CHAPTER 1:

A Woman's Home Is Her Castle 1
An Introduction to the "R"-Rated Guide to Home Repair

CHAPTER 2:

The Big Screw, or There Must Be Fifty Ways to Use Your Hammer 7
A Guide to Tools and Their Uses

CHAPTER 3:

The Story of O 31
Organize Before You Start

CHAPTER 4:

Taking the Plunge, or Fondling Fixtures 39
Learning How to Handle Your Plumbing Needs

CHAPTER 5:

If Gypsy Rose Lee Could Do It 101
Stripping, Spackling, and Painting

CHAPTER 6:

Come On, Baby, Light My World 143
Electrical Repairs and Rewiring

CHAPTER 7:

Drilling Is My Passion 169
How to Put Up Shelves and Other Drill Uses

CHAPTER 8:

I'd Rather Lay a Tile 181
Installing, Repairing, and Replacing Vinyl and Ceramic Tile

CHAPTER 9:

It's Better Than Collagen 209
Furniture Refinishing

CHAPTER 10:

Oh, Just Stick It In, Already! 231
Setting Up and Wiring Your VCR and Stereo

CHAPTER 11:

Is That a Wrench in Your Pocket, or Are You Just Glad to See Me? 247
How to Talk to Repair Workers, Contractors, and Other Servicepeople

CHAPTER 12:

Get a Load of That Woody! 257
Building Your Own (Projects You Can Really Do)

CHAPTER 13:

Cleanliness Is Next to Bossiness 279
Making It All Perfect

CHAPTER 14:

Cocktails, Anyone? 283
The Last Roundup

Acknowledgments

The authors would like to thank our wonderful agents, Bonnie Nadell and Ken Neisser, our patient and understanding editor, Suzanne Bober, Rick Garza, the friendly neighborhood plumber, James Kelly for his words of wisdom, and the ladies from our focus group, Diane, Ginta, Lesli, Susan, Penny, Joan, and Ingrid.

How many men does it take
to screw in a lightbulb? . . .
<u>None!</u>

THE MODERN WOMAN'S GUIDE TO HOME REPAIR

A Woman's Home Is Her Castle

AN INTRODUCTION TO THE "R"-RATED GUIDE TO HOME REPAIR

Women don't know their way around a toolbox. Well, that's right—isn't it? I mean, that's what we've always been told and that belief has caused us to throw countless dollars down the drain (once it's been unclogged), wait for hours for servicemen who never show up, and argue endlessly with spouses and boyfriends over when they're going to take care of that "simple" little shelf for us. ("Arguing," by the way, is our word for what they call "nagging.")

Well, in this book, we are going to dispel that myth once and for all and let you have a few laughs in the bargain. Never again will you have to face a dishwasher that isn't cleaning well, call a repairman only to be told that you should switch from powdered to liquid detergent, and then write a check for $75 for that little pearl of wisdom. Banish forever the scornful sneers you see on the faces of the salesmen at the Home Depot when you ask for "the little thingy that goes in the whatsit next to the round hole." Forget about standing by helplessly while the water level in your toilet gets higher and higher until it runs all over your new Maud Frizon pumps.

This book contains simple, step-by-step instructions that will help you identify your home repair problems, choose the right tools to combat them, and ultimately, fix almost all interior areas of your house all by yourself. And, since there are some things that, no matter how handy you are, you shouldn't attempt to fiddle with, we will let you know when your problems could use some professional help. Incidentally, dealing with that professional help can be a problem on its own, so we'll give you hints on how to talk to the "pro" once he arrives. We've even included three easy-to-follow plans for home improvement projects you can do by yourself and then tell friends you spent thousands getting a decorator to do them.

Before we go any further, we think we should take a moment to introduce ourselves. We are Jeni and Joan, two reasonably attractive (if you don't count the splintered fingers and paint-stained nails), divorced women who, presently, own our own homes but who have been renters and wives (although not necessarily at the same time). We are also women of varying skills when it comes to being able to do things around the house so, in case you think that this book is only for the gifted, rest assured it is not. You see, Jeni is, by far, the more experienced of the two of us, having been known to build her own deck, paint her entire house, and rewire her den without so much as breaking a nail, but Joan . . . well, to put it kindly, Joan is a novice. Oh, sure, she'd put up a few pictures and even was known to climb up on a ladder . . . once, but let's face it, she was much more "tool-ly challenged" than Jeni.

See, what happened was that the condo Joan lives in was going through some heavy-duty repairs and, since she works out of her house, she was the one forced to deal with the contractors and repair people who came traipsing in and out with their measuring tapes, estimates, tight jeans and T-shirts, and . . . stop! We're getting carried away here, but you get the picture. Needless to say, poor Joan was out of her league—at least when it came to the tape measures and estimates. So, she decided it would be a good idea to learn a few things before she continued. Her desire to learn was also hastened by a minor accident that occurred in her guest bathroom: the towel rack fell off the wall. Now, that may not seem earth-shattering to you, but on the day that Jeni showed her how to install a new one, Joan found religion. To put it simply, before this event, Joan had never known that the towel racks and toilet paper holders that came with the place could be replaced. Well, once she learned that, she decided to replace them all, and then there was no stopping her. Doorknobs, shelves, lighting fixtures—the whole world was one giant Tinkertoy and, when she was finished, Joan was a repair junkie.

Hungry for new things to fix, she went in search of any information she could find but, alas, Joan soon discovered that all the books on the subject were written in the foreign language of men's-speak. One look at the overly technical diagrams and dry descriptions and her eyes started to glaze over and she began to dream of piña coladas in warm, tropical climates. At last, humiliated, she confessed her plight to Jeni and, together, they decided to write a book of their own—one designed for women everywhere, women who want to be empowered to tackle the job of home repair with enjoyment and without intimidation.

The next thing to do was to decide on the proper approach for a work of such great importance. After considerable thought, they decided to combine the unknown and formidable task of home repair with something that was familiar and enjoyable to women in general and to themselves, in particular: SEX.

The result of all this thinking is the book you now hold in your hands. Yes, indeed, this volume contains detailed instructions on how to repair things that go wrong around the house down to what tools you will need to use and how hard each task is to do. But it doesn't stop there. *The Modern Woman's Guide to Home Repair* also includes dozens of helpful tips for things you can do to improve, individualize, and beautify your home, condo, or apartment while making it work in a more organized and attractive manner. Simple and inexpensive ideas like changing bathroom and kitchen fixtures, marbleizing a staircase, installing track lighting, and building a designer closet are much easier than doing your taxes or getting your kids to remember to clean up after dinner—and these tasks are much more rewarding. You will find that everything in the book is designed to help you save time and money and will also give you a real sense of satisfaction and independence. There's so much that you can accomplish by yourself.

Now, as we mentioned, we want this book to be something you can enjoy as well as learn from, so we have added an extra benefit. You'll not only get to handle tools and fix things, you'll also have the last laugh doing it. After all, in this day and age when we women have long since proved our ability to hold our own with any man, it is still hard to have the last word when, after you tell him to get out, you then have to call him back and say, "Wait . . . before you go, can you fix my sink?" After reading this book, you can chase him out with nary a backward glance. Hey, maybe he'll even have to call you the next time his toilet starts overflowing. On second thought, is that what we want?

Fine, fine, fine you're thinking. But what does this have to do with sex?

Well, to be fair, this isn't really about sex, per se; it's more about men, in general, and how they view our role in the home repair arena, in particular. This book is jam-packed with amusing and true anecdotes of experiences we and our friends have had along the way, whenever we either asked our mates to do something around the house or, God forbid, tried to do it ourselves. These experiences range from the sublime to the ridiculous: husbands whose idea of a useful tool is their right index finger (to dial for the repairman, of course) to the real Mr. Fix-Its who refuse to listen when you say that it really is necessary to turn off the main power switch before attempting to exchange your cheesy brass chandelier for the new one he just bought which is in the shape of the spaceship *Enterprise*. As they say on TV, these stories were inspired by "actual events."

We hope that by the time you finish our book, you will be empowered to hold your own with contractors who think that, just because you are a woman, you can't possibly understand your way around a power drill. You will be able to rally against the boyfriend who, having finally put in the new counter in your kitchen, becomes so obsessive that he follows you around with a sponge in case you make a mess while stirring spaghetti sauce. And you will be able to run circles around the hardware salesman who, thinking you're a real dummy, uses pig Latin to describe how to change a washer under your sink while trying to cop a feel as he reaches around to show you exactly how to hold a pocket wrench.

Yeah, we hear you, but what about the SEX part? Well, you've got us there. We just threw that part in to get your attention. Sorry. However, for those of you who are in a permanent relationship, home repairs just might turn out to be the kind of hobby you and your mate can do together. It could even be an added bonus for your whole relationship. The possibilities are endless. We heard of one woman who got so fed up with asking her husband of ten years to do some chore or other that she got out his tools and finally did it herself. When he returned that night, she was waiting for him, wearing nothing but his well-equipped tool belt and a self-satisfied smile. From that day on, she never had to ask him to do anything twice.

I guess you could say that what makes our book different and unique is that the information is told from a relatable, female point of view. It uses *our* kind of language and assumes nothing. In other words, it explains in plain, nontechnical English exactly what you need to do to make something work. Remember, we're all down the same drain here, ladies, so take solace in reading the humorous tidbits which are sprinkled liberally throughout. You'll laugh at the images of grown women up to their julietted nails in lubricating grease. You'll cry at the tender moments ripped from the true stories of women who are fed up with being told to "step aside and let ME handle it," and, finally, you'll rejoice as you unite behind the rallying cry of "Handle this, BUD." When it's said with a hammer in one hand and a glue gun in the other, we have found it to be most effective.

So, are you ready? Well, what else can we say? . . . Bob Vila, eat your heart out!

The Big Screw, or There Must Be Fifty Ways to Use Your Hammer

A GUIDE TO TOOLS AND THEIR USES

Equipment is everything. Can you imagine Picasso sitting down to paint and then discovering that he only had one brush and fourteen tubes of blue? Come to think of it, that might be where the Blue Period came from, but, for us mere mortals, we can't do the job if we don't have the right tools for it. The best way to make sure you are prepared for all emergencies is to assemble a **TOOLBOX.**

When we asked our friends if they had a toolbox, we were amazed at the variety of answers we received. Most women had some rudimentary tools which they kept stuffed in a drawer in the kitchen along with string, those wire ties from supermarket vegetable bags, paper clips, matches from way too many happy hours at way too many singles bars, and swizzle sticks from the last office Christmas party when they got drunk and made a pass at the messenger from the mail room only to find out that the hunk in training was the nephew of the CEO. All those items might be useful and hold fond memories, but they have no place mixed in with the tools of this trade. In this chapter we're going to show you how to set up a basic toolbox.

The topics we will cover include:

1. Which tools you should own
2. How different tools are used
3. How to choose a good tool
4. How to substitute common household items for tools in a pinch
5. How to organize your tools

The right tool for the job makes a huge difference. Whatever you're doing will be easier, faster, and usually give better results if you have the right tool. Almost everyone has a hammer, a screwdriver, and a couple of nails lying around, but if you're going to start repairing things, you'll need a few additions.

THE STAPLES

Like putting together a food pantry, having these items is the bread and butter of your repair work. Below we have listed, on the left, the essential tools you should have and, on the right, the items you should add as you go along. In other words, the left column is for those of us who know how to throw a hamburger on the grill and the right column is for Julia Child.

BASIC:	ADDITIONS:
Hammer	
2 flat screwdrivers (small and medium)	Additional sizes
2 Philips screwdrivers (small and medium)	Insulated handle
Small jewelers' or sewing machine screwdrivers	
Cordless screwdriver	
2 adjustable wrenches, 8 and 10 inches,	
Allen wrenches	Set of open and box-end wrenches
3/8-inch variable-speed and reversible drill and drill bits (cordless)	
Pliers: regular and channel, vice grip pliers	Needle-nose pliers
Saws: hacksaw, electric jigsaw	Circular saw
Combination square with level	4-foot level
Combination wire-cutter tool	Circuit tester
Straightedge	
Utility knife	
Putty knife, 3- to 6-inch spackling knife	
Spackle, wood patch	
Electric tape, masking tape, Teflon tape, duct tape	
20-foot metal tapemeasure	
Sandpaper (various grades), sanding block	

Liquid plumber, *WD 40*, or
   other silicon lubricant
Wood glue   Clamps
Pencil, chalk line
Nail set
Paintbrush, toothbrush
Goof-Off paint remover
Anchors, picture frame holders,
   screws, nails, washers, nuts
Heavy-duty extension cord
Flashlight
Staple gun
Wonder bar for removing nails
   and opening cans
   (Don't use a screwdriver!)
Wax for coating screws
   (Don't use soap; it can absorb
   water from its surroundings,
   causing rust.)
Dust mask (air filter mask
   if you are using any toxic
   solvents, paints, etc.)
Safety goggles

Now, before you gulp at the length of the list, don't panic. You don't have to rush right out and buy all of these things at once. Tools generally are acquired over time and as needed. Buying a basic kit will help as most contain the minimum number of tools you will need and you can shop (did we just say "shop"? See, we told you this was something you'd be good at) for the others at your leisure.

Choosing Quality Tools

As in all areas of life, you pay for what you get. Tools are not meant to be disposable items, so a general rule of thumb would be to buy the best quality you can reasonably afford. Look for name brands and ask salespeople what they'd recommend. If you see a special that advertises eight screwdrivers for the price of one, don't assume that the screwdriver fairies are smiling down on you. Assume that you will be throwing away the eight screwdrivers after a few uses.

HAMMERS

First, let's start with something we're sure you are familiar with: the basic **hammer.** Now, up 'til this point, your only experiences with a hammer probably involved those times you tried to hang up a picture or, if you ever lived in Manhattan, your extremely aggressive method of ridding your kitchen of roaches. Well, we're here to tell you that you have only scratched the surface of hammer-dom.

Hammers come in a wide variety of sizes and shapes, each designed for a different use. They range in size from 10-oz **finishing** to 32-oz **framing**. These weights refer to the weight of the head only and do not include the handle. Generally, the lighter-weight hammers are used for delicate finish work, the heavier for framing. Their handles can be made of wood, fiberglass, or solid steel, with each type having pros and cons. A wood handle absorbs more shock than solid steel but can break easily, or the head may become loose. Solid steel is heavy, doesn't absorb much shock and, in our opinion, doesn't have any advantages, so it's not really high on our hit parade. Tubular steel and fiberglass handles, on the other hand, are both light *and* strong. There are some hammers currently on the market that are made from newer, more space-age materials, but they can be pricey so, unless you're thinking of turning pro, they're probably not worth the cost.

Most home repairs can be accomplished with a 16-oz *curved claw handle* (it's easier to remove nails with curved claws than with straight ones). Once again, the choice of handle is really a matter of individual preference and comfort.

A WORD OF WARNING: Never buy a hammer made from cast steel. Melting the steel to cast it weakens the steel by breaking up the natural grain of the metal and can make it a dangerous item to use. Imagine trying to hit a nail and having the head fly off and hit your nosy neighbor between the eyes? Hmm, on second thought, that might be a good defense in a murder case: "But, Officer . . . my hammer just attacked him!"

SCREWDRIVERS

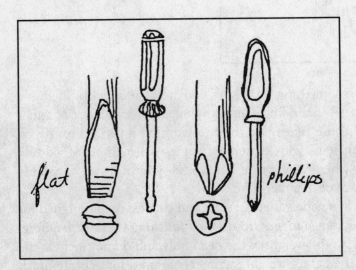

The two basic types of screwdrivers are *flat head* and *Phillips*. The one you need to use will be determined by the design of the screw you are using. This is not hard to figure out, as the pictures above show. Ultimately, you should have several sizes of both types, but you can start out with two sizes of each kind. Some screwdrivers come with exchangeable heads which makes them very handy, indeed, since the heads are stored in the handle of the screwdriver so you are, basically, carrying them around with you at all times. Just pop the old head off and put the new head on as the need arises. Ah, if only that technique worked as well with the men in our lives.

Before you use a screwdriver, it is important to match not only the style of the head to the screw but also the size, as well. Using a driver head that is too small can result in damaging the head of the screw, making it impossible to get it out.

Tip #1: Taking It Off

If you have stripped a screw, take heart. There's a new product called **Screwgrab** (my, my, my, you should see the look on Joan's face) that will help. You just put a drop on the tip of the screwdriver and it bonds to the screw as you press down. Presto, chango.

Remember, politically correct or not, a woman's hands are, by and large, smaller than a man's so all tools may not work equally well for you. Before you buy a tool, test the grip and make sure that it feels comfortable. The basic hold you would use on the handle is akin to shaking hands in a vertical position. (Actually, there is a better way to describe it, but we'll save that for the "X"-rated version of this book.) Handles come in a variety of materials, from plastics to metal, and you might eventually develop a preference.

Jewelers' screwdrivers are really handy when it comes to dealing with small nails on doorknobs, light fixtures, and other decorative items as well as fixing your sunglasses after the dog sits on them and makes them go all out of shape. (Joan's dog, Pepper, has made an Olympic event out of that little trick.)

WRENCHES

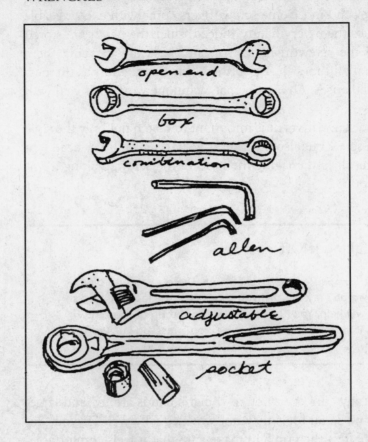

The basic purpose of a wrench is to enhance your ability to grip something firmly and to apply leverage. As we mentioned above, our smaller bodies need all the extra leverage we can get. We guess a good way to think of wrenches is as a way to add weight to your body without having to go to Jenny Craig afterwards.

When buying wrenches, look for those made in drop forged steel for the extra strength they provide. Your basic needs will be met by getting an **adjustable type** wrench in both 10-inch and 12-inch models.

Tip #2: It's All in the Wrist

When something is hard to turn or in order to increase your leverage, tighten one wrench onto the object, then tighten another
onto the handle of the first wrench. Use the second wrench to
turn the first.

Allen wrenches, which are hexagonal steel tubes bent at a ninety-degree
angle for gripping, are nice additions to your tool inventory but, when
you use them, make sure that you insert the wrench into a matching in-
dentation in the head of a screw object in order to turn it or it could go
flying free of its mark.

DRILLS

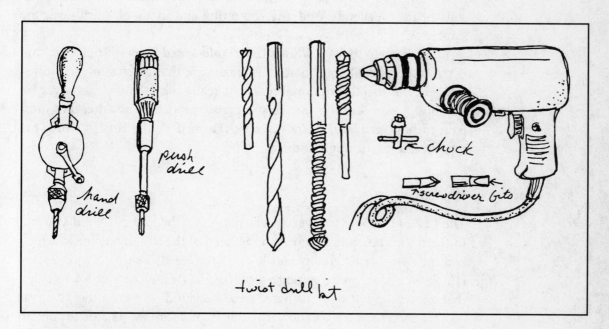

Joan has just discovered drills and seems to get a particular pleasure out
of walking around the house with one in hand looking for something to

use it on. While most of you don't need to go that far, you are probably only familiar with the drill as a tool for making holes. In a later chapter, we will show you that there are lots and lots of other things you can do with a drill, but its primary purpose is to make holes.

Drills start at around $35 and go up from there. They come in two basic types: **cordless** and **plug in.** The cordless variety will handle most of your basic household needs but, as it doesn't have the power of a standard plug-in drill, you will need to have the latter if you plan on doing any heavy-duty or outdoor drilling. *A hint:* It's best to keep your cordless drill plugged in all the time so it will be ready to use when you need it but, if you don't have room to do that, remember to give yourself enough time to charge it FULLY before you start your work. There is nothing worse than being in the middle of something and having your drill sputter and die. To give you an idea of what it would be like, remember what happened when you and your significant other were going at it, hot and heavy, and you just *casually* mentioned that your mother was coming to stay for the weekend? Well, the sputtering and dying of a drill feels the same way.

To get back to tools, a **3/8-inch, variable-speed reversible** electric drill is the most versatile but, here too, make sure that the size of the drill is one you can handle comfortably. Those really big mothers may give you the most power, but they are very expensive and so heavy that they are a pain to hold in place. We're not sure the thrill of the drill is worth the whiplash injury it might induce.

Drill Bits

The size of the hole you get is determined by the size of the bit you put in the drill. The bit is attached to the head of the drill by a chuck, which is a little key that tightens and loosens the head. Joan is forever losing chucks so she suggests getting a drill that has a built-in slot for it. If not that, you can put it on a chain and wear it around your neck the way your mother used to make you do with your front door key. It's a better buy to purchase a set of bits rather than going out and buying them individually. Bits, too, come in a variety of materials that determine their durability so price will likely be a determining factor here, too. We like the titanium bits that are a bit more expensive but have less of a tendency to break off mid-job and which last a really long time.

Bits are categorized not only by size but also by function, so it's important to use the right type of bit for the job at hand (e.g., wood for wood, masonry for brick, etc.). Each bit is designed differently and specifically for what it has to do. A masonry bit has a large head so as to be able to enter the brick with maximum power. The shank of a wood bit is designed so the wood shavings are pushed backwards out of the hole as you go along. If you use the wrong bit for the wrong job, you might not only damage the drill and waste time, but also ruin the surface and material on which you are planning to work.

Tip #3: Size *Does* Count . . .
Sizing Drill Bits to Fit the Hole

We searched, but there seems to be no magic way to automatically know what size drill to use with what size screw. Sometimes you'll get lucky and the packet of anchors or box of screws will state the size you need to use, but mostly, it's a question of trial and error and letting your eye be your guide. One word of warning, however: When in doubt, start with the smaller drill bit and work your way up. As with dieting, it's easy to enlarge but almost impossible to reduce.

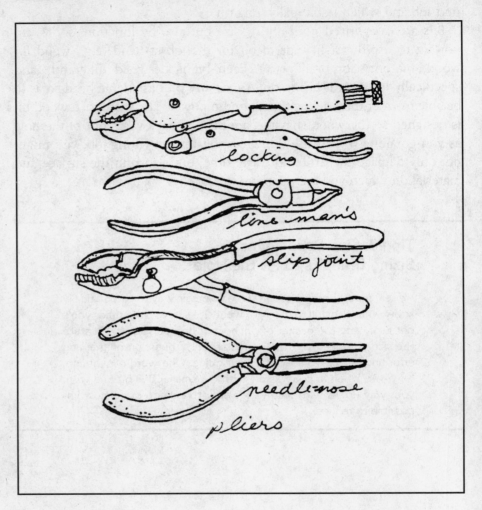

You are probably familiar with the basic plier shape but, here too, their specific uses vary according to design and style. In general, however, pliers are used for gripping and pulling. (Picture a tooth being yanked out of your mouth at the dentist's office, and you'll have a rough idea of what we're talking about.)

Vise grip pliers clamp onto the object and are particularly useful because they lock in place and can increase the power of your grip. **Needle-**

nose pliers are small, pointed, and useful for getting in tight places or gripping small objects.

Tip #4: A Tip from the Pros

To increase your leverage, you can tighten a wrench onto the handles of the pliers and use it to turn them.

SAWS

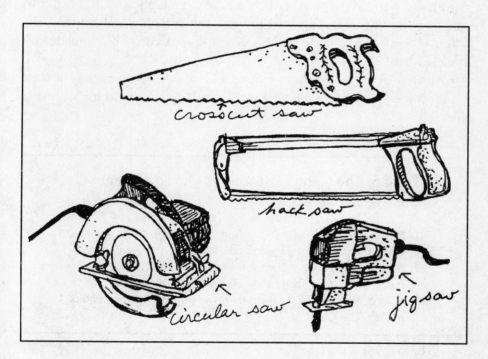

crosscut saw

hack saw

circular saw

jigsaw

If the first thing that comes to mind when you think of a saw is the image of ugly ole' Paul Bunyon having his way with the trunk of a tree, you need to get out in the world more, girl. Nowadays loggers come wearing Ralph Lauren and with a mouth full of gleaming white teeth (at least they do in the beer commercials we watch). We know that the idea of using a saw can be intimidating to some women because of the sharp teeth and the rather forceful action you must use to make it work but, used intelligently, a saw can be a very handy item to learn how to master.

The two basic types of saws you should start out with are the **hacksaw** and the **jigsaw**. A **hacksaw** is a hand-held, nonelectric saw with a small, thin blade that is very useful for working in tight quarters. A **jigsaw** is an electric saw, with a small blade that moves straight up and down. You can add a circular one when you get more confident with these two. A **circular saw** has a blade, usually 7 1/4 inches in diameter, that spins and, among other things, can make much deeper cuts than a jigsaw.

When choosing blades remember that when Little Red Riding Hood said to the wolf "What nice teeth you have," his reply was "the better to eat you with, my dear." Thus, the more teeth per inch your blade has, the better and smoother the cut will be. (We know, it's corny, but it made you smile, didn't it?)

CAUTION: Using a saw does require a lot of care so if you are the least bit squeamish or among the well manicured, don't even think of trying this.

Tip # 5: The Hand Isn't Always Quicker Than the Eye . . . Safety First

1. Move your hand as far away from the saw blade as possible, while still maintaining the hold on whatever you are cutting.
2. When cutting wood, don't cut through a knot. These are incredibly dense and can cause the blade to bounce back.
3. Always wear safety glasses when working with power equipment.

KNIVES

In addition to a good **utility knife**, a **Swiss army knife** with its collection of multipurpose pocket tools can be extremely useful in a pinch. It's not a bad idea to keep one in your purse for emergencies (Jeni does, although it boggles the mind to imagine the kinds of emergencies she gets into) or to use when you garden. Just remember, it's easy to cut yourself on the blades when opening them so watch your fingers, please.

Putty and **spackling** knives have wide, flat blades for applying and blending putty and spackle and are definite "musts" for any kind of repair work you do to walls and floors. (By the way, you should keep a fresh container of wall spackle on hand to help with those drilling goof-ups. We say fresh, as the spackling material does tend to dry out over time especially if the container is not airtight. It can be reconstituted, however, with the help of a few drops of water.)

NAILS AND SCREWS

Here's a trick question: What is the difference between a **nail** and a **screw**? Give up? See, Jeni, Joan told you she wasn't the only one who didn't know. Throughout all of history women have been confused about what exactly these two little items actually do. To put it simply, a **nail** works by pushing the fibers away from itself and creating a friction that will hold it in place when hammered in—kind of like the feeling you get when you put on a pair of control-top panty hose. **Screws**, on the other hand, trap the fibers in their threads, creating a much stronger attachment. (Imagine the control-top panty hose with rubber suction cups and you get the picture.) Nails are faster and cheaper and are probably what you'll need most of the time, but if you need greater gripping power or think you'll need to undo something at a later date, use a screw. Once again, choose the proper size *and* style nail or screw for the job you're going to do. In other words, the screw might look right but, if it doesn't fit, your entire project might fall apart.

There are various types and sizes of nails and screws so, below, we will try to give you a thumbnail (sorry)-sized look at their infinite variety.

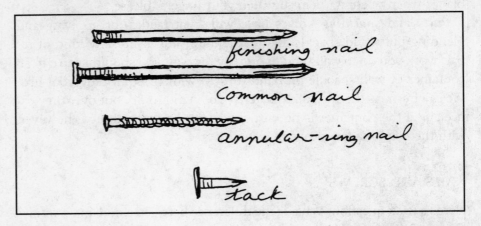

Common nails: These are probably the nails you're most familiar with. They have flat heads that are wider than their shanks and are used for general carpentry work. Sizes range from 1 to 6 inches long. Common nails can be bought with a regular finish or "galvanized." Galvanized simply means that they have been dipped in a coating that resists rust.

Finishing nails: You can recognize finishing nails by their small heads, which are almost the same size as their shanks. They are used for carpentry, cabinetmaking, and any type of work where the final appearance is important. They run from 1 to 4 inches long and do not come galvanized.

Annular-ring nails: This type of nail almost looks like a screw except that, while a screw has one long spiral cut out of it, annular rings have a series of ridges that grab onto the wood, thus increasing the resistance to pulling out. They are commonly used in man-made panels made of composite materials. (A composite is made of lots of small fibers pressed together.)

The only project in this book that requires annular rings is in the section on tiling. We call for them if you need to prepare your floor for the tiles by laying a sheet of plywood over your old floor.

Tip #6: Tacky, Tacky, Tacky

Don't get confused between a nail and a tack. A tack is much shorter and lighter and is commonly used to attach carpeting to wood. Their tips are very sharp, so as not to pull carpet fibers, but they pull out easily so don't use them for other things.

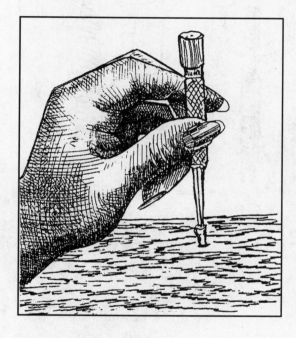

Nail sets are tapered metal cylinders designed to aid in driving a nail all the way into the wood without leaving hammer marks. You place the small end of the nail set directly on the nail and hit the top end with a hammer, thereby saving walls and delicate little hands.

Screws

Screws have come a long way since being invented by the ancient Greeks. (When Jeni asked Joan why *that* piece of information was important, Joan told her that once she had lost a game of Trivial Pursuit over that seemingly obscure fact. And since Jeni knows how Joan *hates* to lose at anything . . .)

In the following section, we will describe only a few of the many, many different kinds of screws on the market. Just so you know a screw when you see one, remember that a screw is a fastener with a pointed spiral thread cut or pressed into it. They are generally under 4 inches in length and vary as to the size and shape of their heads. (We'll let you fill in your own joke here.)

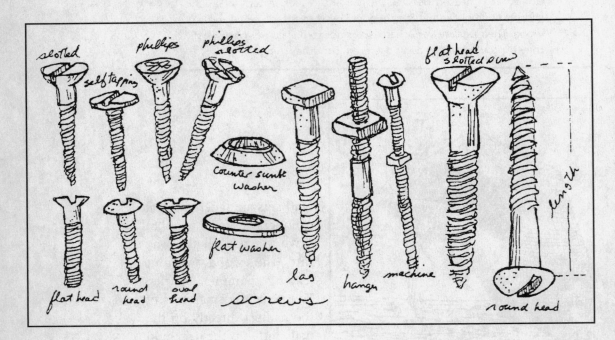

There are three basic screw head types:

FLAT: designed to be recessed into the wood.

ROUND: for use on materials that are too thin for countersinking.

OVAL: used to attach metal to wood.

Screws were originally made with a single slot in the top; however, since a screwdriver could easily slip out of the slot, other designs were added that give a better hold. These include: the **cross slot** (Phillips), **hexagonal** slots, and **square** slots. We recently found some nifty tamper-resistant heads in a variety of configurations but, for our purposes, the simpler common screws are fine.

Screws are sized by length and gauge. The gauge is a measure of the thickness of the spiral thread and is a number from 1 to 20, with the most commonly used gauges being 4 to 10.

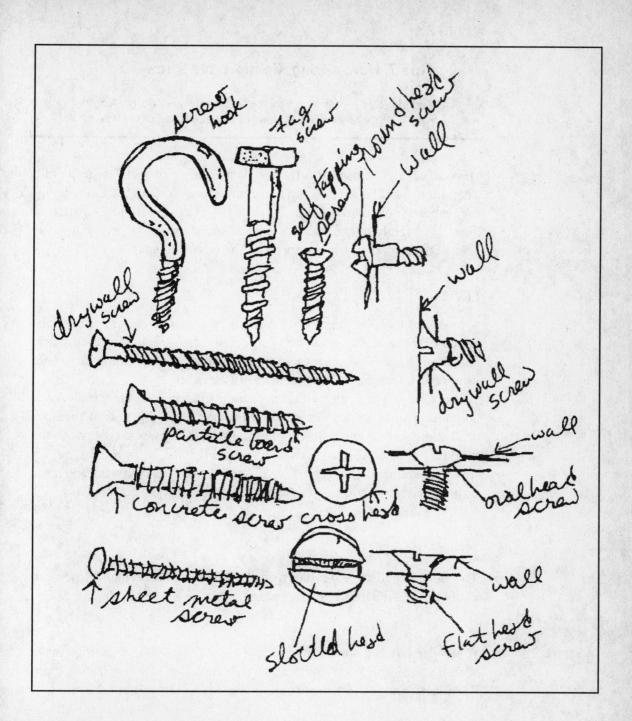

Tip #7: Have a Long, Comfortable Screw

A longer screw is stronger than a wider screw, so go for length over width, every time—but, you knew that already, didn't you?

Drywall screws are specifically designed to attach Sheetrock to a wall. They should not be used to carry structural loads, or any loads like hanging cabinets or bookshelves. They will effectively hold a panel of Sheetrock tightly to the wall but cannot withstand strong perpendicular forces (shear forces), which can cause the screws to snap.

LEVELS

A *level* is a tool designed to tell you when something is precisely horizontal or vertical. We guess you can call it a lie detector for your work, and it is essential when you are putting up shelves or doing any other kind of work where measurements must be exact.

It is kind of like a ruler with one or more glass vials in the middle, each containing special liquids and an air bubble. Place one end of the level against the surface and adjust it until the air bubble is exactly between the marked lines on the glass vials. This is a level line.

We recommend you get at least a 2-foot level. The larger the level, the more precise and reliable your measurements will be.

MISCELLANEOUS

The items listed here we like to call "mother's little helpers"; they can really make a difference in your work.

A *wonder bar* is a small crowbar that makes removing nails a lot easier than if you simply used a hammer. It also can be used to pry things apart, open cans, and for leverage when you need to lift something.

A **chalk line** is a piece of string wound on a spool filled with chalk. Use it when you are laying tile and need to delineate spaces or when marking straight lines over longer distances than a straightedge (ruler) would cover. At one end of the chalk line there is a hook that you pull out and attach to a fixed surface in order to hold it in place. Once secured, you pull the line a few inches away from the surface and let it snap back in place, leaving a line of chalk.

Anchors are a must for your tool and parts collection and are used primarily when you want to hang pictures or put up shelves. We will describe them more fully in the chapter that deals with drilling and shelf construction.

Cleanup products are available for all types of materials. Again, we will go over them in the later chapter on cleanup, but the general caveat here is to use the proper product for each job. If you use paint remover on your carpet, for example, you might remove all of its color unless the substance is specially formulated for that purpose. (The look on Jeni's face is screaming "Tell me you didn't?") By the way, this reminds Jeni of a party she gave when she was seventeen—we'll be kind and not say how many years ago that was. Anyway, her mom was out of town at the time so, Jeni decided to take advantage of her absence and entertain a hundred of her "closest" friends. Unfortunately for her, the crowd got a little rowdy, so the next day, Jeni took to her hands and knees in a frantic race against the clock to remove grenadine spills from the brand-new turquoise and white shag carpet before her mother returned. (Turquoise and white??? Sounds like a little grenadine might have been an improvement.) It didn't work, but little Jeni did live to tell about it.

Who'd a Thunk It? . . . Unorthodox "Tools"

We women are so ingenious that it was interesting to see what some of our friends came up with as tools just from items commonly found around the house. Here's a list that we know we will be constantly adding to:

1. *Rubber bands and ponytail holders* to get a better grip on slippery tool handles. A friend of ours swears you can even use a ponytail holder as a temporary washer to fix a sink, but we have our doubts!
2. *Bobby pins* to hold things in place while you finish your job.
3. *Nail polish remover* in place of paint remover for small spills.
4. *Candle wax* can be melted and used to lubricate screws for easier insertion.
5. *Toothbrushes* used in this context are not meant to appease the Dental Hygiene Association but are great for cleaning out grout, smoothing down spackle, brushing away wood shavings formed during drilling, and for a myriad of other cleanup uses, as well.

ORGANIZING YOUR TOOLS

Whether you have a garage, a closet, or a special area in a room, it really does help to keep everything neat and together. Not only will it make it easier to see what you have and what you need, but if a pipe bursts in the middle of the night, you won't be forced to scrounge around in a panic, dumping out the contents of your drawers in search of your wrench.

Your first thought will probably be to start out with the familiar red metal box. While it is inexpensive, it is also small and you will soon outgrow it. Unfortunately, when Jeni decided to splurge on a really big box, instead she got one that was too heavy and awkward—and the bruises on her shins are witness to that sad tale. A better idea is to set up a separate area in which to store your tools and then, as the need arises, transfer what you will use into a smaller toolbox and carry *that* easily and comfortably to your work area. By the way, in the last couple of years, manufacturers have come up with new designs and materials

for toolboxes which make them lighter and softer so you won't have to schlep the carrying case, either. A canvas-and-leather gardener's tote can also be handy because it has lots of pockets. We do know one woman who bought a Louis Vuitton bag for hers, but she's just a big old show-off.

Jeni, who has a world-class collection of tools, finds that since she never won any prizes for neatness, she often forgets to put things back in place after she has finished with them. This leaves her with a massive problem when company is coming as she tries to hide hammers under cushions and sequester pliers behind piles of dishes. If that is your problem, too, you might be tempted to just dump everything in one big drawer and deal with it later. Need we mention that that is a *really* bad idea which will lead to more work and frustration later? A better way to go is to avoid drawers altogether and use shelves, instead. Jeni puts coffee cans on the shelves and then stands all her screwdrivers in one, hammers in another, etc. Cutlery holders work well in this regard, too. You can keep washers, nails, screws, etc., in **glass jars** or those **multidrawer organizers**. Joan uses plastic handy boxes with lots of little compartments. She likes these because you can store them flatly, one on top of another. Jeni gets fancy when it comes to her drill and jigsaw. She hangs them from small bungee cords, one end hooked onto the shelf with the cord looped under the tool and the other hook put through the first one—easy to unhook, easy to put back, and it can double as a piece of modern art.

Throughout the rest of the book we will give you more specific uses for each of the tools and helpful items that we have described above so that you can see how they work in real situations. As you branch out and discover the areas in which you are doing most of your work, you can modify your tool collection to suit your own needs. Just remember, collecting tools can be addictive. We've heard about women who become positively possessed when they discover that their neighbor's collection includes a super, amped-up power drill that they simply *must* have. As with all addictions, our best advice is to take it one "bit" at a time.

CHAPTER

The Story of O

ORGANIZE BEFORE YOU START

Generally speaking, there are two types of people in the world: the organized and the unorganized. We were taught to recognize them from our earliest childhood years. The organized types were the ones who looked upon the first day of the school year as the happiest of their lives. There they sat, their little hands folded serenely over their brand-new spiral notebooks with two nicely sharpened number-two pencils lined up alongside. The unorganized types had only a measly piece of paper on which they could scribble and had forgotten their pencils altogether. As we grew up, however, the lines between these two types of people began to blur, and one type often merged into the other. Thus, you have the person who carefully makes a shopping list and then leaves it on the kitchen counter (Joan) or the one who, painstakingly, reads directions on how to do something and then does it her own way, anyhow (Jeni).

In home repairs, there is room for both types of people, but, we warn you, without real organization, your task becomes more difficult, time-consuming, and expensive. Joan is a perfect example of the otherwise organized person who, somehow, loses her head once she gets near a hammer. One day, she got a notion to replace the bronze light panel over the sink in the guest bathroom with one that was either chrome or mirrored (to match her newly installed chrome toilet-paper and towel holders, natch). She carefully measured the area, noted the number of screws in her present light panel, and hip-hopped off to the hardware store to buy the replacement. Unfortunately, that is where her organizational skills ceased to function! She had failed to take off the old panel first in order to figure out what kind of wiring system went underneath. Had she done so, the poor girl would have discovered that she couldn't just unscrew the old one and blithely screw in its replacement. Instead she would need to disconnect the wires holding the old panel in place and reconnect them to the new attachments. Imagine her surprise when she discovered that she now had a real electrical mess on her hands. She then made the situation worse by attempting to improvise once she had the whole thing exposed. It's sad, really, since, with a little organization, she would have avoided slipping off the vanity she had climbed up on, pulling the towel rack off the wall on her way down in an effort to break her fall, and leaving a severe gash in the wall as the metal pole scraped against it when the rack came off in her hand. A little organization would also have saved her the $65 she had to pay to her chiropractor to get her neck and shoulder snapped back into place following her fall.

The bottom line here is: Plan your task in complete detail before you do anything and then, like Patton at Calais, stick to it.

THE PLANNING COMES IN THREE PARTS

1. Assess what needs to be done.
2. Make a list of all necessary supplies.
3. Make a list of all steps needed for the completion of the task.

Assessing What Needs to Be Done

This might seem really obvious, but it isn't. Just saying "I need to fix the sink" doesn't quite cut it. What exactly do you need to do? Once you have answered that question, you will be able to decide if you should attempt the project on your own or call in a professional.

When you know what the problem is and decide it's something you can tackle successfully, read as much as you can about what the project entails and ask questions, too.

Making a List of All Necessary Supplies

Don't go to the hardware store blindly. This is not the time to see if something is on sale or strikes your fancy. (Actually, this is pretty much what Jeni does, but we make an exception in her case.) Make a note of exactly what you need, how many you need, and the correct sizes. If you are replacing a part, when possible, take the part with you. If you can't, draw a picture of it and show it to the nice person in the hardware department.

Measure carefully, and then do it again before you leave. There is an old carpenter's saying: "Measure twice, cut once." They really do it, too. If you need a length of something and are uncomfortable cutting it yourself at home, get the store to cut it for you. If you do the cutting yourself, buy a little extra, just to be safe.

If you are installing something, read the directions carefully before you start and make sure all needed parts are included. If you need something extra, buy it before you start your work.

Tip # 1: If You Don't Know Where It's Been . . .

If you purchase something in a package that has been opened and then retaped closed, open it while in the store and check to make sure all the parts are included. Mistakes are made sometimes, and you'll save yourself much aggravation and a return trip to the store after you've gotten home and discovered that the final bolt you needed is missing.

Make sure that you have all required tools and that they are fully charged, sharpened, and in operating order.

Making a List of All Necessary Steps

- If you are following written directions, make sure you understand each point and, if you don't, call or go to a hardware store and ask questions.
- Don't leave anything out. This is not the time for shortcuts, and if when you're finished there are some extra parts left over, you goofed.
- Follow safety precautions. Turn off the electricity if you are working with wire and currents. Turn off the water before doing plumbing repairs.
- Check to make sure that you have all parts with you *before* you start work. There is nothing worse than being halfway through a project and discovering that the tool you need is in another room.
- Bring cleaning products and rags or towels with you to the site. If something spills, clean it up then and there before it causes more damage.

If you are working in an area out of your reach, make sure that you have a safe way to reach it. Check your ladder or footstool for strength and security. Do not climb on furniture or balance yourself on ledges. This is home repair, not tryouts for Le Cirque de Soleil.

If what you are doing requires more than two hands, wait till you have help; do not try to contort yourself into two positions at once (see previous note on Le Cirque de Soleil). By the same token, take into account that women, generally, weigh less than men and the size of their hands is considerably smaller. Leverage is the key to doing any job if you don't want to end up in traction for six weeks, so make all necessary accommodations before you have that monster wrench in your hands with not enough strength to turn it.

If you are taking something apart, make a diagram of what it looks like before you do so.

Stay calm and whistle while you work.

MAINTAINING AN ORGANIZED WORLD

1. Regularly check your tool chest and supplies to make sure you replenish anything you have used up.
2. Check the status of your tools and do any resharpening or replacing of wornout tools before you are going to need them.
3. Keep an eye on the circulars that come with your Sunday newspapers as they often advertise sales at home repair stores. A sale is a good time to add to your tool stash. Also, if new items are being shown, you might be able to get an in-store demonstration of their use. In fact, the Home Depot chain has regular demonstrations on topics like tiling, gardening, and painting at many of their stores.

The final tip comes in the way of the "an ounce of prevention" school of thought. Keep a first-aid kit on hand and make sure it is well supplied with Band-Aids, antiseptics, cotton, tape, etc. We don't want to sound like old worry warts, but even the most skilled home repairer has an occasional slip, and a finger dripping blood is not the best way to make a good impression on a new date.

Now you are ready to approach your tasks (Joan's father used to call them "chores," which always made her feel as if she should be looking for a pitchfork to help load on the hay). The rest of the book is separated into sections about repairs and improvements around the house. Use the chapter on tools as a reference when approaching each project and apply what you learned here to organize your work. Okay? Well, ladies, you've done your prep work and you've been swell, so go out and make us proud of you. Remember, you're not just doing it for yourselves, you're doing it for legions of women everywhere who are fed up with waiting for some man to come and save the day. Ready, aim, SCREW!

4

Taking the Plunge,
or Fondling Fixtures

LEARNING HOW TO HANDLE YOUR PLUMBING NEEDS

We believe that the bathroom and kitchen are the two most important rooms in the house. Think of it this way: anything you can do in the bedroom, you can do anywhere (frankly, it's often more fun that way), but if your bathroom or kitchen is out of commission . . . well . . .

In this chapter we want to help you identify plumbing-related things that can go wrong in those two areas and what you can do to make them right again. We also want to go on record here as saying that there are some things that we don't think you should mess with and we'll list those, too. By and large, however, when it comes to *fixing leaky faucets* and *showers, unclogging drains*, and *stopping running toilets*, you are woman—hear you flush!

Plumbing is not all drudgery and Cinderella time, however. There are some really neat things you can do to upgrade and personalize your bathroom and kitchen areas through fixture improvements that are not too expensive, relatively easy, and can make you feel like your bathroom represents the real you. Wait a minute, is that something we should be exposing to just anyone who wants to take a leak in our boudoir? Sure, why not—if they don't get the hint any other way, maybe a shiny new faucet will do the trick.

And, for the bonus round, we're going to be giving you a lot of helpful little tips along the way as well as some information about bathroom safety and household products that you might not know. So, check your chapter on tools, make up your list of tasks to accomplish, put on a John Coltrane album, and plunge, baby, plunge.

DEPENDING ON THE KINDNESS OF STRANGERS (OR WHEN TO CALL A PLUMBER)

If any of the things below happen, you need to call in the guys who do this for a living:

1. *Ruptured mains*: These are easily detected by either a sudden drop in pressure or the appearance of a thirty-foot high geyser in your backyard that is attracting the attention of camera-wielding tourists

who became lost on their way to see Old Faithful in Yellowstone National Park.

2. *Appliances*: If your dishwasher, garbage disposal, or washing machine is on the blink, call the manufacturer for a repairperson in your area. We do, however, have some tips on things to check before you call the plumber. They are listed toward the end of this chapter.

3. *Blocked Main Drains*: The way to tell if your drains are backed up is to check *two* fixtures, the toilet and the bathtub or shower. The reason for this is that, unlike the sink, these are the two lowest points in the house. If the toilet won't flush and water sits in the tub/shower, your main drain line is blocked and the repair will be beyond your meager powers to cope with it. If only one looks plugged, you're in luck since only one fixture is affected and you can probably handle it yourself.

TO MARKET, TO MARKET . . .
GOING TO THE HARDWARE STORE

This'll be easy. Before you start repairing, you get to do something you're already good at—shopping. Now, we know that hardware stores can be very intimidating places. They're usually filled with lots of men wearing tight T-shirts and well-worn jeans who leave a faint aroma of sweat in their wake. Wait a second, these are places you've been avoiding?

Well, the trick to success in the wonderful world of tools is to have a sense of purpose, some basic knowledge about what you want, and the courage to ask questions about what you don't know with a reasonable sense of authority. Giggling and pointing is not the best code of conduct. Okay? Got that? Well, here we go.

1. When possible, ***take the broken part*** (washer, bolt, screw, or whatever) with you. Trying to describe it from memory or act it out might be fun if you're playing a really strange game of charades, but, frankly, in the middle of a busy parts department, you'll look like an idiot.

2. When that is *not* possible, ***make a drawing***, identify any parts you can, and measure carefully. Don't worry about trying to make it three-dimensional. Line drawings are fine. This isn't Miss Cutler's sixth-grade art class so no points are taken off for neatness, but

don't try to do the Salvador Dalí version, either. Keep it as simple and realistic as possible.

3. If size and spacing are important, **measure** and then measure again. That's the way the pros do it. A quarter of an inch can be the difference between success and freaking out your kid by letting loose a torrent of ugly curse words when you see that what you bought doesn't fit. Besides, you don't want to make more trips to the hardware store than are really necessary (not unless the salesman looks a whole lot like Mel Gibson and, trust us, he seldom does).

4. Speaking of salesmen, unless you know exactly what you need, ask for help. Standing around and letting your eyes glaze over as you look at a display of 264 types of washers is just plain silly. Chances are, you'll never find it yourself and, after forty-five minutes of looking, you might be tempted to grab a nearby customer and hold him hostage in exchange for the proper information. **Ask intelligent questions** and you'll get helpful information.

WORD TO THE WISE: Beware of shortcuts. Learn it the long way, first. We heard about a poor woman who thought she would get really cute and try cutting a few corners on the installation of a washer only to have the whole thing blow up, literally, in the face of her future mother-in-law. Of course, she did make the situation much worse than it needed to be when she cracked up at the sight of the mascara running down the older woman's face after the accident. We guess the moral to that story is, always buy waterproof.

5. **Assume nothing**! Here's a tragic story that shows how even our own Jeni Munn can fall victim to 20/20 hindsight.

"Several months ago, I was watching a how-to show. Subject: toilets that continually run. Now I have never wanted to go near a toilet that needed fixing. I figured that toilets were majorly ucky and when they broke it meant it was time to call the plumber. But, at $9 versus $100, it was time to take the plunge. So, off I went to the hardware store, where I got my repair kit (a new flush valve) and, with much confidence, proceeded into the breech. I thought I was so clever. I turned the water off, dismantled the toilet, and installed the new kit. When I put everything back together, however, my sixth sense told me something wasn't right. Okay, the biggest hint was really the fact that the tank was furiously rocking back and forth.

"Undaunted, I double-checked my installation, but it seemed okay, so, I shrugged it off and turned the water back on. When the water in the bathroom started reaching my ankles, I decided something was wrong. A tail-between-my-legs trip back to the store and a snickering salesman later, I learned that when you remove the two bolts, washers, and rubber gaskets in order to take a tank off its base, unless the gaskets are very new, they will almost always need replacing. Now, this little tidbit wasn't mentioned in the directions because it has nothing to do with the flush valve—it's just a 'side effect.' But no one at the hardware store had deigned to mention this and I didn't know to ask. So, now when I embark on a repair, I always ask 'Is there anything else I should be prepared for?' "

Thank you, Jeni. Thank you for sharing.

6. If, when you enter the store, the salesman is surrounded by other people in need of help, ***don't be intimidated***. It's just like ordering a drink at a bar. Look the salesperson in the eye and patiently, but expectantly, flirt like mad. If that doesn't work, start crying. That always works for Joan, although Jeni prefers a more direct form of intimidation: she carries a loaded weapon.

Tools of the Trade

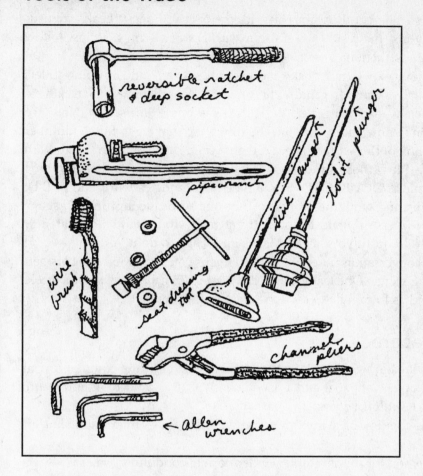

DON'T BE SUCH A DRIP, OR HOW TO FIX LEAKY FAUCETS

There is nothing worse than being right in the middle of an intimate moment with a loved one when you are distracted by the "drip . . . drip . . . DRIP" of a leaky faucet. (Talk about using the "rhythm" method.) This particular variety of coitus interruptus, alone, should be enough of a reason to study this part carefully.

The other reasons include:

1. Once you get the right parts, it's pretty easy, honest! Leaks are usually just the result of worn-out **washers** or **O-rings**, so just follow the instructions.

2. In our experience, leaky faucets and showers and running toilets usually occur after midnight, on Sundays, or when you have an especially bad hangover. We'll call this one Munn's Law. Now, we don't know about you, but the thought of having to find a plumber at any of those times is not one that sends us leaping in the air with joy. Plus, those times were especially designed by the plumbing genie as DOUBLE TIME. You'll be mainlining caffeine, and he'll be whistling while he works to the tune of beaucoup de bucks. So, save those dollars for something really important like that new DKNY outfit you saw at Macy's and learn to do it yourself.

3. A conversation note: No matter where you live, good water is getting scarce. One leaky faucet can waste 175 gallons of water a week. And as for a toilet, you don't even want to know!

Be Prepared!

Clear an area to work on. If it's the kitchen sink, clear the counter next to it. Have a piece of paper and a pencil handy. Gather your tools and **locate the water shutoff valves.**

This is the first of many times you will hear this jolly refrain: **shut off the water.**

The reason for this is simple. Under normal conditions, water is always in the pipes, ready to burst forth at the slightest opportunity, so if you were to dismantle the faucet without shutting the supply off, water would come shooting out in your face, sending parts flying, which can be dangerous, and cause a bad-hair day, which, as we all know, can be disastrous. In case we didn't make our point, the accompanying flood of water on your floor will make Noah's deluge look like a tiny leak.

Most sinks and toilets have individual shutoff valves. If they don't, you will need to locate the main supply valve, which is usually near the water meter. (In any case, it's a good idea to know where both your gas and water line shutoffs are should an emergency arise.)

Let's Do the Twist (How to Shut Off the Water)

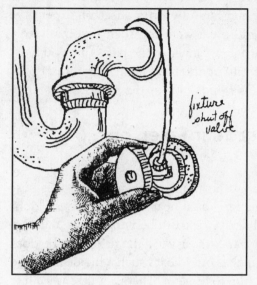

fixture shut off valve

Think of this as just another faucet, like an outdoor hose. Turn the handle clockwise until it's snug, but don't try to tighten it with brute force.

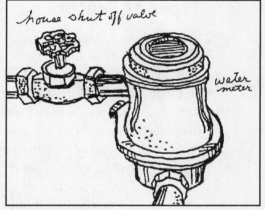

house shut off valve

water meter

This should also be turned clockwise, or, if it is a lever, move handle so that it is perpendicular to the pipe.

Once you have shut the water off, open the faucet or flush the toilet that you are working on. This gets rid of the water that's left in the pipes.

Now get ready to **take the faucet apart.** Remember that pencil and paper we told you to get? Well, this is where you're going to need it. We've all heard the story of the guy who took an appliance apart, fixed it, put it back together, and found he had an "extra" part left over. (Here's a hot tip: There *are* no extra parts.) So, unless you are experienced at this, you will probably not remember how everything went together in the first place.

Also, again according to Munn's Law, it is usually right when you have everything spread out around you that: a) the cat comes flying through the room trying to escape an imaginary demon; b) the doorbell and/or phone rings, and in your haste to answer it, you knock over the antique Ming vase your grandmother left you; or c) if you live in California, as we do, an earthquake will strike and all the king's horses won't help you put the place back together again. For those of you with kids . . . well, I'm sure you get the picture. Therefore, in order to avoid confusion, when you take something apart, lay it out carefully on a sheet of paper and make a note and a stick drawing of how it went together. If you are feeling cocky and think you know the actual names of the parts that you have just cast asunder, you can try identifying them by name (e.g.; *washer, O-ring, nut, balls*), but we caution: this step is not for the novice.

Faucet, Prepare to Meet Your Fixer, or Types of Faucets

You are about to learn more about faucets than you ever thought was possible or even desirable, for that matter. You'll hear words that are seldom used in mixed company and you'll learn the truth behind the big, dark secret that men have held on to for years: It's easy! So the next time he does something around the house and makes out like it's such a big deal that he deserves a reward for doing it, tell him to forget it. That is, unless *you'd* like to share in that reward yourself and then—watch out, honey, the fleet's in!

There are three types of faucets, **cartridge, ball type**, and **compression**. Since the repair methods and parts needed are different for each, it is important to know what kind of faucet you have. This is not necessarily apparent just by looking at it from the outside, so we'll begin by taking the faucet apart.

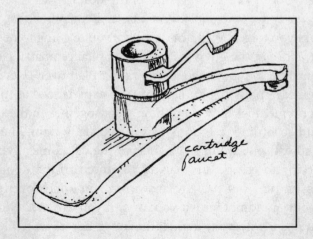

cartridge faucet

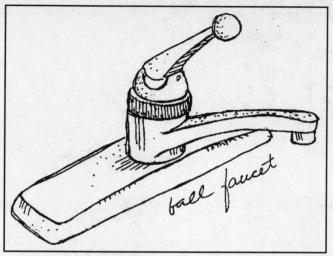

ball faucet

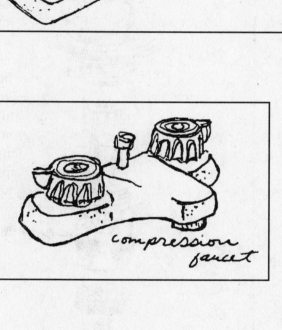

compression faucet

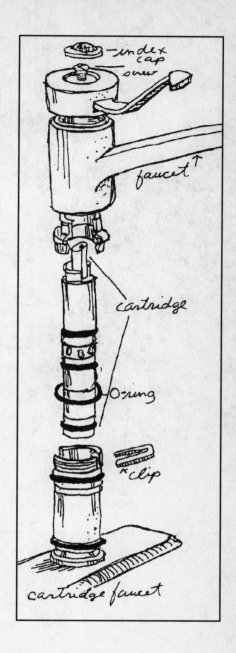

index cap

screw

faucet ↑

cartridge

O-ring

clip

cartridge faucet

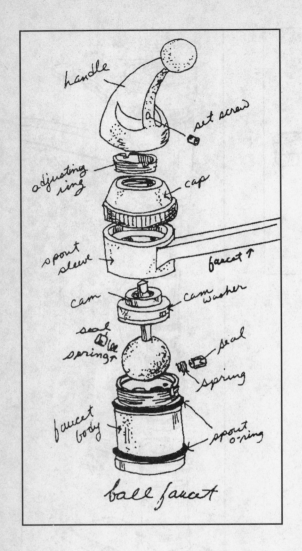

handle

set screw

adjusting
ring

cap

spout
sleeve

faucet

cam

cam
washer

seal
springs

seal

spring

faucet
body

spout
o-ring

ball faucet

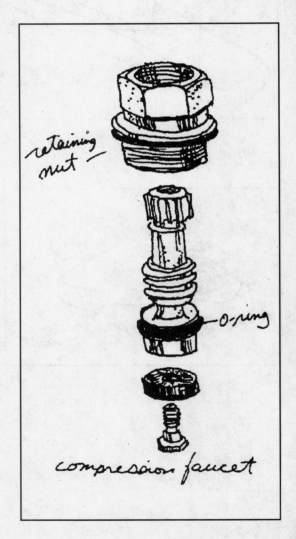

retaining
nut

o-ring

compression faucet

Once you have identified your faucet type, double-check that you have the right tools for the job. If not, add them to your list and proceed to the hardware store. Again, take the part with you, especially washers and O-rings. A washer that is just a little bit too thick or a smidgen too small won't work and you'll pay the price for it later.

STEP-BY-STEP INSTRUCTIONS: FIRST YOU PUT YOUR TWO KNEES . . .

Fixing Cartridge Faucets—Disc Type

Materials needed: a cartridge unit (which contains all the mechanical parts)

Tools needed: Allen wrench, screwdriver

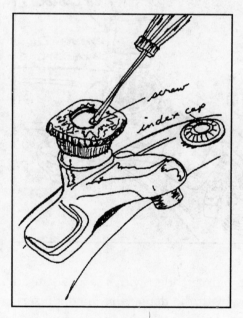

Pry off the **index cap** with a screwdriver and remove the screw you see there. This will allow you to remove the **faucet handle**.

The next thing you see will be a **handle insert.** In the back is a **setscrew.** Loosen this with an **Allen wrench**, then remove the handle insert. Turning counterclockwise, unscrew the **dome cap** and remove it.

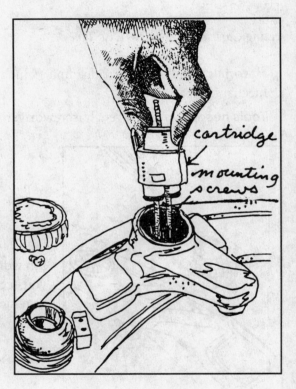

You will see the **cartridge** is held in place by two **mounting screws**. Remove them and lift out the old cartridge.

Working backwards, replace the old cartridge with the new; insert mounting screws and tighten; follow with the **dome cap, handle insert, setscrew,** and **faucet handle;** and cap it all off with the **index cap.**

Fixing Cartridge Faucets—Sleeve Type

Materials needed: a new cartridge, plumber's grease

Tools needed: screwdriver, pliers (channel-type and needle-nose), O-ring

Remove the ***index cap*** and ***handle screw***. Remove the ***handle*** by lifting the lever up, then, holding the handle by the ***collar*** at the base, not the lever, gently lift the handle off. There is a ***retaining nut*** under the handle; if you feel a resistance, wiggle the lever a bit more to make sure it's all the way up. That should release it from the retaining nut.

Next, with ***channel-type pliers,*** remove the retaining nut. You may find that there is a ***grooved collar*** underneath the nut; if so, remove this also.

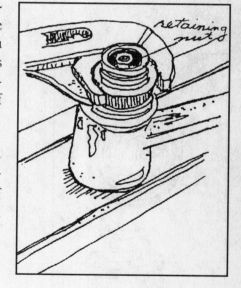

With a pair of ***needle-nose pliers,*** pry the ***retaining clip*** off the top of the ***cartridge***.

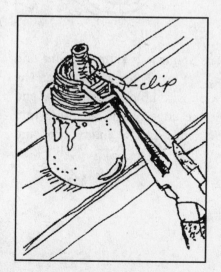

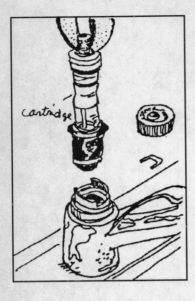

cartridge

With the **channel-type pliers,** grip the top of the cartridge and pull straight up. If it is stuck, apply WD 40 or other penetrating oil and gently rock back and forth until loose. Do not use brute force; you may damage the faucet. Insert the new cartridge and reinstall the retaining clip.

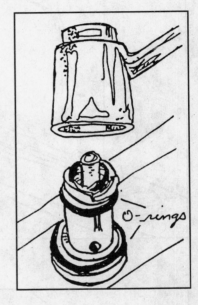

O-rings

Now you need to lift off the **spout.** This may take some twisting as you pull, but again, brute force is not what's needed. Cut off the old **O-rings.** Spread plumber's grease on the new O-rings and slip into place.

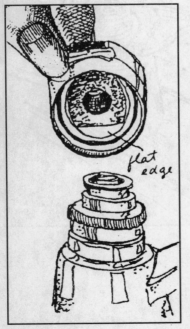

flat edge

Working backwards, replace **spout** and **retaining nut** and **lever.** If you look inside the lever you'll see a **flat edge.** The trick to getting the lever back on is to hold it at an angle, and then slip this flat piece over the edge of the retaining nut. Screw the **handle screw** back in, add the **index cap,** and you're done.

Okay, are you still with us? You're doing great, you know, and those overalls you picked up at the Gap look absolutely perfect on you. Do they come in any other colors? What, Joan? You're right! We think you deserve a little treat. Now, go to the phone, dial the number of your friendly neighborhood health spa, and book a massage. That way you'll have something to look forward to as you plunge (no pun intended) deeper into the strange world of faucets.

Tip #1: Just Let Me Slip into Something More Comfortable . . . Getting the O-Rings Back On

In our experience, what goes off must, eventually, go back on. Usually this part is harder than it looks or, maybe it just seems that way because you're fed up with the task and just want to open a bottle of Pinot Grigio and veg out. Well, as our heroine Blanche DuBois said to Stanley, "Preserve your soul in patience" and suck it up!

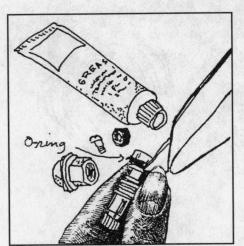

Now, to get these little suckers back in place, take a small flat-blade screwdriver and roll the ring up the shaft. Place the blade of the screwdriver next to the object you are trying to put the new O-ring on. Roll the O-ring back down the shaft and then over the top of the object.

Continue rolling and maneuvering until the ring is properly placed. Holding the O-ring in place with one hand, pull out the screwdriver. (If you have trouble with this one, ask your teenage daughter to help you out. She learned a similar technique in her sex education class lecture on "how to use a condom.")

Fixing Ball Type Faucets

Materials needed: You will need to buy a kit that has a ball, cam, cam washer, valve seats, and springs. (For some peculiar reason, these are often packaged in two separate kits. Ask a guy; it makes no sense to us.)

Tools needed: screwdriver, channel-type pliers, utility knife

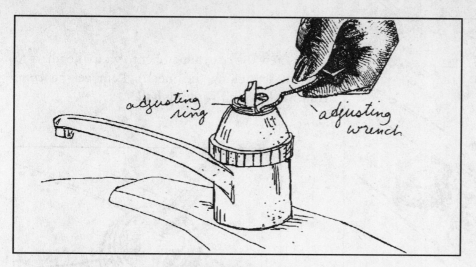

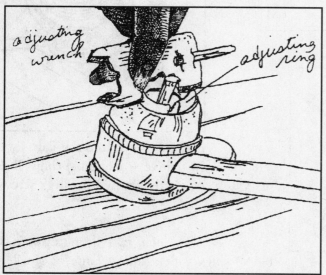

At the base of the handle is a *setscrew*. Using an *Allen wrench,* loosen the screw and remove the *handle.* Underneath this is an *adjusting ring.* Try tightening it with an *adjustable wrench* or *channel-type pliers.* This may cure the leak, so reattach the handle, turn the water back on, and see what happens. If it still leaks, you will need to turn the water off, remove the handle again, and proceed.

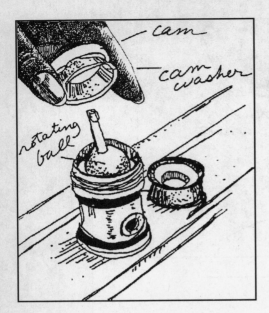

Unscrew the *cap* (remember to wrap the pliers to prevent scratching the metal). Remove the *cam, cam washer,* and *rotating ball.*

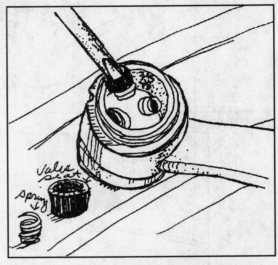

Looking down into the faucet, you will see two *valve seats* and *springs.* Remove these by gently prying up with a screwdriver.

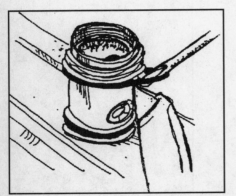

Next, remove *spout* by twisting upward. Cut off the old *O-rings* with a *utility knife* or small, very sharp pointed scissors. Replace with new *O-rings* that you have coated with the plumber's grease. At the base of the spout is a *plastic slip ring* that the faucet sits on. It's a good idea to replace this, too. Put the spout back on, pushing down until it's securely in place against the plastic slip ring.

Working backwards again, install new *springs* and *valve seats,* as well as a new *rotating ball, cam washer,* and *cam.* Screw the cap back on and reinstall the faucet with the *setscrew.*

Fixing Compression Faucets

Materials needed: You will usually need a new washer and O-ring. You may also need a new screw, if the old one is worn out. (Joan was heard snickering at this.) A new valve seat may also be necessary. Plumber's grease.

Tools needed: screwdriver, utility knife, adjustable wrench, seat wrench, and a seat dressing tool (These are sold in packs of four and are sized and shaped differently to fit a wide variety of sinks. Why they can't make them all the same, we don't know, but one will fit.)

As usual, we start by trying to undo the **screw.** You will soon find that, as in life, a screw plays a big part in the exciting world of plumbing. If there is an **index cap,** pry it off with a screwdriver and then, holding the handle, undo the screw. Remove the **handle** by lifting straight up. If it sticks, get out the good old WD 40 and rock gently. The idea is to work the oil into the crevices so it can do its job.

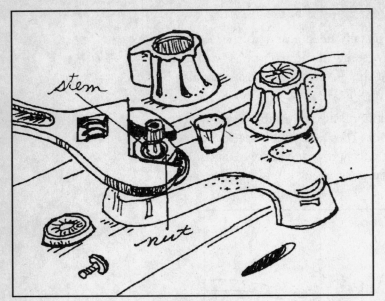

Next, loosen the **retaining nut** with an **adjustable wrench.** When loose, it's easier to unscrew it by hand than with the wrench, so remove the nut, then pull out the **stem.**

At the bottom of the stem is another **screw,** remove it and the **washer** underneath it. Put in a new washer (again, it's critical that the washer be an exact match). If the screw looks worn, replace it also.

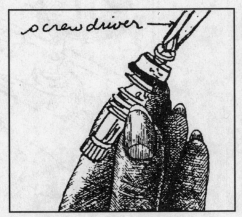

Cut off the old **O-ring** with a **utility knife** or sharp scissors. If you have difficulty maneuvering around the old O-ring, pull it out slightly with strong tweezers or carefully push the blade of a small screwdriver underneath the ring, then cut. Remember, don't hold the stem in your hand while cutting the **O-ring.** Place on a counter or other hard surface, hold at one end, and cut in the opposite direction from your hand.

Install a new **O-ring** and smear plumber's grease on **stem, retaining nut,** and the **handle socket.** We're sorry, but there is no tool you can use to do this. Just stick your fingers in and pull out a good size glob. *Eeeww!* Joan, in particular, finds this disgusting, but she was the kind of little girl who didn't like to play in the mud—so take that with a grain of salt.

After you've gotten all the parts well lubricated, check the valve seat by running your finger around it. If it shows signs of wear, is pitted or corroded, try liposuction. No, seriously, you'll have to replace it, as follows, before reassembling the faucet.

Lift and Tuck . . . What to Do If Your Valve Seat Needs Fixing

You have two choices when it comes to fixing a valve seat: replacing it or resurfacing it. This is also called "dressing" the valve—not the kind of dressing we usually do, of course, but, then again, you wouldn't want Mother to see a naked valve seat, would you?

Materials needed: guide disc

Tools needed: seat wrench, dressing tool kit

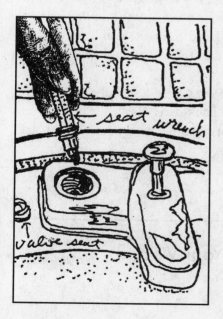

To replace the valve, use a **seat wrench** to remove the old one. Insert it and turn counterclockwise to remove. To install a new one, turn clockwise.

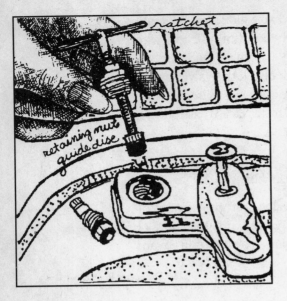

ratchet

retaining nut
guide disc

Occasionally, you will not be able to remove the old valve seat and therefore must dress it. For this you will need a *dressing tool* and a *guide disc* of the right size. After attaching the guide disc to the dressing tool, insert *through* the *retaining nut*. Gently tighten retaining nut. Press tool lightly and turn *ratchet* clockwise. When the tool turns easily, the seat has a new surface.

Working backwards, whether you've had to replace the seat or not, re-install the *stem*, add the *retaining nut,* screw the faucet *handle* back on, and replace the *index cap*. If you resurfaced the seat, you'll need to remove the *retaining nut* before inserting the *stem*, then screw the nut back in place and reassemble as above.

All right! You're done. Wait a minute . . . not so fast. Put the cap right back on that bottle of scotch and come back here. Hark, we hear a faint dripping sound coming from the vicinity of your bathroom shower that just might have your name on it.

TUBS AND SHOWERS

If April Showers Do Come Your Way . . . Repairing Leaky Showers

FIXING SHOWERHEADS THAT DRIP

Materials needed: new washer (possibly), Teflon tape

Tools needed: scissors

If the drip is from the showerhead, you don't need to turn the water off. Unscrew the showerhead. You will see that the threads of the stem are wrapped in a white or pink tape. This is **Teflon tape**. If there isn't any, you may have already found the problem. Check the washer. If it's worn, replace it.

Before screwing the showerhead back on, you will need to retape the threads. Remove the old stuff. Then cut a piece of tape about four inches long. Holding it in place at one end, wrap the tape around the threads *clockwise*. This will form a seal, preventing leaks.

Fixing Faucets in the Tub or Shower

If *only* the hot water faucet is leaking, go to your water heater. There will be a valve on one side where the cold water comes in. Turn this off. Back at the shower, run the hot water until no more comes out. If both the hot *and* cold taps leak, however, and the **escutcheon** is round, you will need to turn the water off at the mains. If however, the escutcheon is **tear** shaped, there will be individual shutoff valves easily accessible behind it. This is most frequently found in apartment buildings, condos, or other multiple-family dwellings and helps prevent an uprising among your neighbors who were in the middle of their showers when you decided to do some home repairs. We don't know about you, but the sight of the overweight man who lives next door screaming and dripping water all over your floor while he tries to keep his towel tied around his waist really pushes the idea of "love thy neighbor" just a little too far.

REMOVING AND TURNING THE WATER OFF BEHIND TEAR-SHAPED ESCUTCHEONS

Remove handle the same way you would for a **compression faucet** on a sink. Undo the **setscrew** and remove the **escutcheon.** In the wall behind it you will see your water supply pipes. You'll see a little valve where it looks like you could use a flat screwdriver to turn it. This is called an integral stop, and you do indeed use your trusty screwdriver to turn it 90 degrees, shutting the water off.

REPAIRING THE LEAK

Materials needed: O-ring, washer, packing washer

Tools needed: screwdriver, reversible ratchet, deep socket

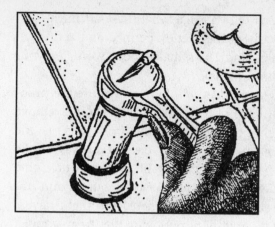

Using a **reversible ratchet** and **deep socket,** remove the **bonnet nut.** If it won't budge, get out the good old WD 40 or liquid wrench. Apply, wait ten minutes, and try again.

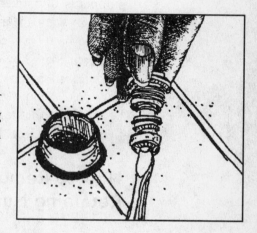

Undo the **stem screw** and replace the **washer** under it. Remove and replace the **O-ring** and **packing washer**. Lubricate all parts with plumber's grease and reassemble.

GLUG, GLUG, GLUG, OR CURING CLOGGED DRAINS

Once more Jeni turned to Joan and asked, "Do we really have to do drains? They're icky." Joan looked up from doing her exercise routine and said, "Yes, we do." Jeni wanted to ask her, "Who's the 'we'?" but Joan was counting so loudly while doing her scissors kicks that Jeni didn't want to interrupt. Actually, it was intimidating. Joan works out *six* days a week. Jeni, on the other hand, freely admits to being a schlub. So, here goes. Jeni *does* draw the line at unclogging toilets. "We do have to leave a few things for men to do, after all."

Let's start with the easy things first:

Draino and other chemical cleaners: BAD IDEA! They all say they're safe for pipes, the environment, etc. They lie; they're not. They are extremely caustic, generate heat, and can damage pipes and enamel surfaces. Plus, the small print doesn't tell you that what these chemicals *will* damage is rubber (as in your washers and section connectors) and when the rubber goes, you have leaks, and leaks make more work for your plumber. (*Hmmm*, do we smell a conspiracy here?)

Next on the list are plungers. A plunger will frequently cure the problem. But in order to get the full force of the plunger, you should remove the drain stopper first. Since eight times out of ten the problem is that the stopper is all gunked up and you should routinely clean it anyway, you're going to want to know how to remove it. Many lift straight out. Some need to be turned counterclockwise, and a few have a retaining nut underneath that should be released. Now, this is where you might have a tendency to get lazy and try to fix it without removing the drain stopper, but don't. We know. You are all busy women, but the drain stopper might be the thing that makes a difference between success and a glop of gunk flying in your face. It's your choice, but don't say we didn't warn you.

How to Remove a Drain Stopper That Has a Retaining Nut

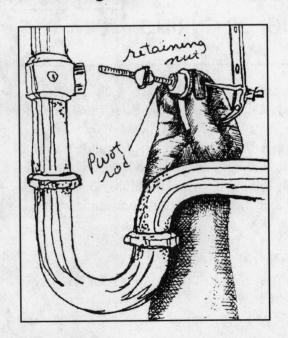

The **stopper** should be raised and in the open position. If you look under the sink, you will see a **rod** attached to the drainpipe. On this is a **retaining nut,** which you should first unscrew, then pull the rod away from the pipe. This will release the stopper so you can then pull it out of the sink. Now you will have the great good fortune to discover exactly what the stopper has been hiding. So that's where all that thinning hair was going!

When you clean all the gunky stuff off the stopper, inspect the **rubber gasket,** and if it's worn, replace it. Now, use your method of choice to unclog the drain. Then, replace the stopper, but if there is an "eye," make sure that it is aligned with the **pivot rod.** Insert the rod through the drain hole and retighten the retaining nut.

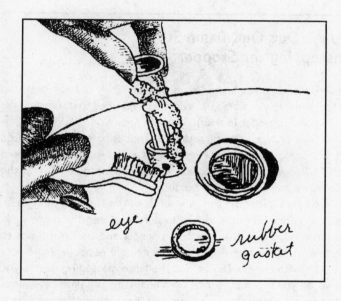

Tip #2: Suck It Up . . . Using a Plunger

Did you figure that this was one area you thought you could get through without instruction? Well not so fast, Ms.-I'm-getting-the-hang-of-this-pretty-easily. As with everything else, there's a right and a wrong way to the art of plunging. So, here goes:

1. Stuff rag in the overflow opening.
2. After you position the plunger, run a little water over it. This will help form a seal.
3. Plunge away!

Tip #3: Out, Out, Damn Stop . . . Unstopping the Stopper

If every time you wash your expensive and frilly teddies, bras, and undergarments you come back after ten minutes to discover them all clumped together looking like mere rags, your basin is not retaining water. If, when you raise the stopper to let out the water, it drains so slowly that you could read *War and Peace* in the interim and you know the drain isn't clogged, then the problem is that the stopper isn't set at the right height.

Take a look under the sink. If your sink is housed in a vanity cabinet, push aside all those "gift with purchase" items you got suckered into buying at the Lancôme counter and be careful not to knock over those half-empty bottles of cold remedies from your last bout with the flu. Dig behind the large massaging device you use when you're, *umm*, "tense" (we hear from our plumber friends that that is where a lot of women keep their Mother's little helpers) and you will see that the stopper is connected to the pivot rod by a strip of metal with several holes in it. (You will also make your umpteenth vow to clean out and organize under the cupboard.) The strip of metal is called a ***clevis***. (Clevis is another one of those words that you've never heard before but that will, suddenly, appear everywhere.)

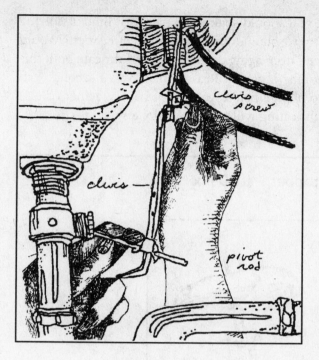

clevis screw

clevis —

pivot rod

If the stopper isn't going down far enough, you need to move the pivot rod to a higher hole in the clevis.

If the sink is still draining too slowly and you see that the stopper doesn't rise up enough, then loosen the screw at the top of the clevis, pull the pivot rod down, and retighten the screw.

Bathtubs

Now for the *tub* stopper. Make sure it is, also, in an open position and pull up the stopper. Peer inside and you'll see a hinged metal arm underneath; this is called the *rocker.* If you've ever done this before (and, if you have, you've been holding out on us, you devil), you'll recognize this as the part you can never quite get back in the hole the same way it came out. (You might be more familiar with it by its nickname, having called it that "damn thingamajig" once or twice before.) Clean the stopper and lay it aside. Next, remove the screws from the *overflow plate* (this is a circular metal disc on the wall of the tub, below the faucet), remove the plate and carefully pull it and the assembly that you had no idea was behind it out from the wall. Clean thoroughly. If it shows signs of age, corrosion, or hard water–salt buildup, you should soak it in vinegar or lime dissolving solution. (Wait! Is this a tip we should pass on to Elizabeth Arden? Would that our skin could be freed from aging as easily.) Now, lubricate both this and the stopper with plumber's grease. Reassemble. Wait a second: Jeni wanted to remind you to **plunge** before you put it back together or else all that dissolving and lubricating will have been done in vain.

Tip # 4: The Stopper, Part Deux

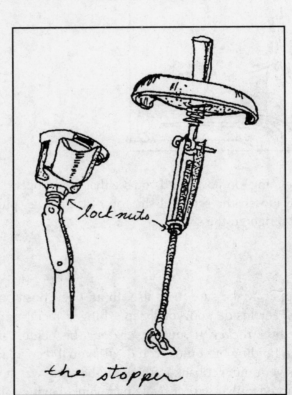

the stopper

If the drain leaks when the stopper is closed, look under the stopper. There is a locknut there; loosen it and screw the stopper down. If the stopper doesn't rise enough and drains too slowly, move the stopper up a little.

Removing and Cleaning the Drainpipe

If you're at this stage in the process, you're really in deep, girl. Taking apart drains is the John Wayne of plumbing chores, so stand tall, Pilgrim. After this one you can belly up to any bar with the best of them because this is what you do if the sink drains are like, totally clogged, and nothing else has worked. Yeah, we know you'd rather just light a match, fling it over your shoulder, and torch your bathroom, but it's a much better idea if you take out the **drain trap** and clean it.

The trap is nothing more than a U-shaped section of pipe, inserted below the sink. It has two functions, trapping debris that might otherwise clog the drain and, because water sits in the U, preventing odors from traveling back up the drain. It is designed to be easily removable for cleaning, but, then again, panty hose aren't supposed to run as soon as you take them from the little egg, so you'll have to be the judge. Also, make sure no one is around when you do this little task. The last thing you want is for anyone to see the private contents of your drain. After all, you should be the only one to know the truth of what lurks down there.

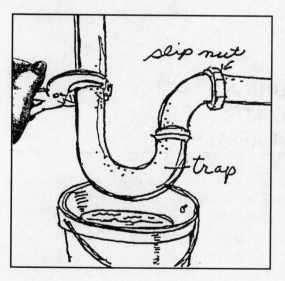

Arm yourself with a bucket, rubber gloves, channel-type pliers and a stiff brush for cleaning. Whistle while you work and put the bucket under the U bend and, using the pliers, loosen the nuts. Finish unscrewing them by hand, then pull out the U bend.

Working over the bucket, empty the trap and clean the inside with the brush. If you are unable to remove the clog, and you can take it outside, try forcing it through with a garden hose. Don't try the hose inside or in the shower because guess where all that goop's going to go. If it remains clogged, replace the U bend with a new one. This may sound serious, but it isn't, honest.

If you have to replace the drain trap, DON'T PANIC! Remember, you are just screwing something back in that you already know how to take out.

IS YOUR TOILET RUNNING? WELL, GO OUT AND CATCH IT . . . OR MASTERING TOILET REPAIR

A broken toilet is no laughing matter. And, like death and taxes, this topic, too, is inevitable—a rendezvous with destiny, so to speak. Come to think of it, toilets should be considered the great leveling device of our society; no matter who you are, you have to use one, so it's a hell of a lot less embarrassing to learn how to fix it yourself than have it explode just when the man of your dreams decides he has to use it for the first time. (Like fingernails on a blackboard or metal foil against old fillings, this is an image that speaks for itself.)

First of all, these items should NEVER be flushed down a toilet:

1. Cotton (this one Jeni's never tried, but evidently Joan has).
2. Any kind of kitty litter (between us we have nine cats, so trust us on this one).
3. Photos of old boyfriends, even after you've shredded them into little pieces.
4. Q-Tips.
5. Paper towels.
6. Sanitary napkins (tampons are okay, but not their applicators, no matter what they say).
7. Any piece of your kid's toys (more Legos and toy Power Ranger figures have been dredged up from the inside of a toilet than you can imagine).
8. Condoms.

With regard to this last item, there is a sweet tale we would like to share with you. This one comes to us courtesy of our favorite plumber, Rick.

It seems, Rick and his crew were called upon to install a new septic tank for a couple of blissfully happy newlyweds. They were thrilled with his work and he went on his way, never thinking that he would hear from them so soon after the installation. Lo and behold, he was summoned there not one month later with complaints that the tank was all stopped up. He went to work on the problem while both husband and wife stood by, biting their nails with worry. What could have happened to put a crimp in their domestic bliss? Suddenly, a clear and buoyant object floated to the top of the tank. Then, another and another until, finally, the septic tank was filled with a flotilla of objects, all bobbing and weaving their way across the surface. What were these objects? Closer inspection revealed them to be condoms and, boys and girls, not just your regular drugstore variety condoms, but ribbed ones, colored ones, and a few French ticklers to boot. Well, Rick was embarrassed and more than a little turned on as visions of the young lovers frolicking in the bedroom leaped through his brain. Then, he looked up and saw that the face of the husband was starting to turn fifteen different shades of red. When he saw

the wife take off for the hills with the husband in hot pursuit, the picture became clear. All at once, Rick remembered that the husband was a traveling salesman and had told him that he had been on the road for most of the past month. Guess the little woman decided to have her honeymoon with another groom.

The moral of this story is very simple: If you're going to cheat, don't trust your toilet to keep your secret for you. Throw the condoms in a trash can, preferably one several miles from your home!

The Care and Feeding of Your Average Toilet

(A quick primer on how they work)

In this section you'll see the following words used frequently:

flapper
float ball
ball cock

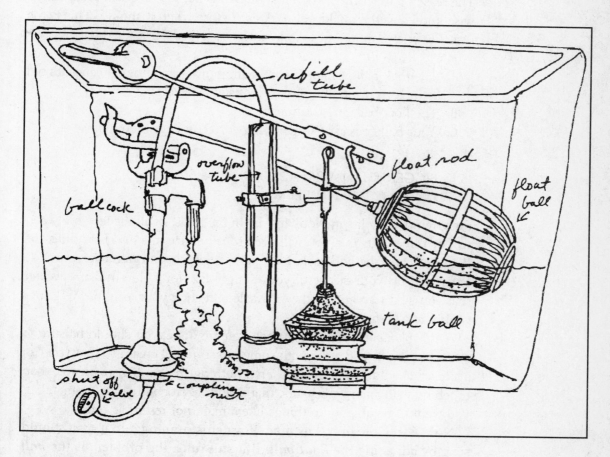

These words do not refer to some weird sexual practice concerning sports stars in the 1920s; they are working parts of your toilet.

When you flush the toilet, the handle moves the **trip lever**, which in turn raises the **flapper** or **tank ball**. Water rushes into the toilet bowl through the hole under the tank ball. As the level in the tank drops, the *float ball* sinks, opening the **ball cock,** which brings in fresh water. The float ball is designed so that it drops enough to open the ball cock just at the point where the tank is almost empty. Thus, fresh water starts refilling the tank and toilet bowl. As this is happening, the tank ball falls back into place, covering the hole and sealing the tank. *Voilà!*

But, as you might imagine, things can go wrong. Timing is everything! The reason a toilet runs when it shouldn't is because the **ball cock,** otherwise known as the intake valve, doesn't close when it should. This is the result of one or more of the following:

A. The tank ball or flapper isn't sealing properly, either because it's old and worn or because it isn't adjusted correctly.
B. The float ball isn't floating right.
C. Your ball cock isn't functioning correctly. (But then, whose is?)

IS IT BIGGER THAN A BREADBOX? . . .
(IDENTIFYING THE PROBLEM)

First, remove the lid and look inside. In the midst of all the ice-cold water will be three parts that you will need to recognize: the ***overflow tube,*** the ***float ball,*** and the **ball cock.** Now, take a deep breath, remove your jewelry, push up your sleeve of your simply fabulous blue mohair sweater that you got at an end-of-the-year sale and stick your arm in. We know, we know—it's freezing!

A little plumbing beauty tip: When you are done, you should be sure to coat your hands and arms with some moisturizing cream so that you can avoid cracked and dry skin. There's nothing that's a bigger turnoff than touching your man with hands that resemble crocodile hide. Remember, you want to be able to do things like a man, not resemble one.

Now, check the ***overflow tube.*** If water is running into it, you should start by adjusting the ***float ball.*** If it still runs, the problem is the **ball cock.**

If, however, you don't see any water running into the overflow tube, look into the bowl. If the water is rippling, the problem is the ***tank ball***. Sometimes you can see that the tank ball is not properly covering the hole and water is running through. It may just have gotten out of alignment. Some tank balls are connected with two chains; one may be loose or tangled up, preventing the ball from dropping smoothly back into place. If so, you can just untangle it and be on your way. We, naturally, always try the easy fix first—but if that doesn't work, we're afraid it's "Abandon hope all ye who enter here."

Fixing the Float Ball

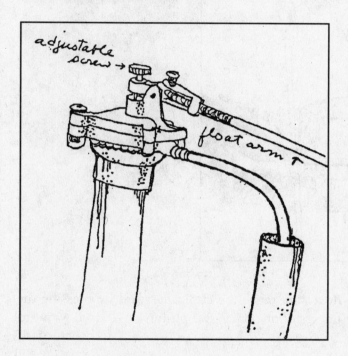

First, check the condition of the *float ball*. If there is water in it, it has a leak and you need to replace it. Since the float ball controls the valve that lets in the fresh water, proper positioning is critical. The higher the float ball, the higher the water level. If it's too high, the *ball cock* will keep trying to fill the tank and it will run into the *overflow tube*. The float ball will not rise to the occasion, and the water will continue to run. The proper water level is about a half inch below the overflow tube. The float ball is attached to the ball cock via a *float arm*. Where this meets the ball cock, there is usually an **adjustable screw;** try turning this. If there isn't a screw or it doesn't seem to move the arm far enough, carefully bend the arm down slightly.

Adjusting the Float Cups

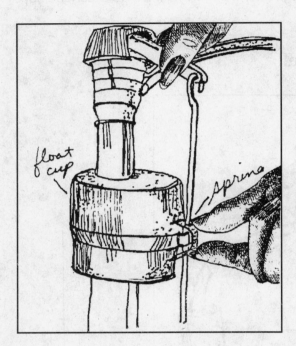

If your toilet has a **float cup,** move the cup downward by pressing the **spring** between the fingers of one hand and pushing the cup downward a little with the other.

Regulating the Ball Cocks

Plumbing is like life—it's the ball cocks that'll get you, every time. Now what, you might ask, is a ball cock? *To put it simply, a ball cock is nothing but the device that controls the level of water in your toilet.*

There are two types: the **plunger** and the **diaphragm** (trust us, we are not making this up).

Plunger Type

Materials needed: washers, O-rings, packing washers
Tools needed: screwdriver

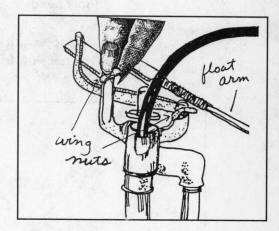

Turn the water off and flush to empty the tank. Undo the **wing nuts** and slide the **float arm** out. Grasp the **plunger** by the top and pull it out.

You will see a **washer** at the bottom and an **O-ring** or **packing washer** in the middle. Remove and replace both with exact matches. Clean the inside of the **ball cock** with Q-tips or paper towels. Reassemble.

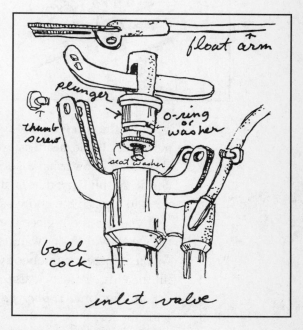

Diaphragm Type

Materials needed: rubber diaphragm, valve plunger OR new ball cock assembly, new rubber gasket

Tools needed: screwdriver, wrench

We don't suppose that by now we still have to say it, but, just in case some of you are slow learners: *Turn the water off.* Good, now flush.

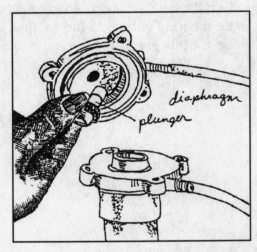

Undo the *screws* at the top of the *bonnet* and lift off the *float arm/bonnet piece.* Underneath is a *diaphragm,* check its condition. By now, we should all know what a good piece of rubber looks like! You should also check the *plunger* that is attached to the bonnet. If it is worn, you may need to replace the entire assembly.

If you need to replace the entire ball cock assembly, look at the base of the tank, where the water supply line comes in. You'll see a *nut* and a *washer* (these are frequently plastic these days). Undo both, then you can lift the entire ball cock assembly out and insert a new one. If the ball cock was resting on a *rubber gasket,* you should purchase a new one, along with the kit.

I've Grown Accustomed to Your Pace . . . Fixing a Leaky Tank Ball by Realignment and/or Replacement

Materials needed: new tank ball kit (possibly), nylon dish pad without soap (optional)

Tools needed: screwdriver

Once again, turn off the water to the toilet and flush to empty the tank. Inspect the **tank ball/flapper.** The rubber should be firm and uncracked. (Stop, we're getting excited!) If not, replace it. Also, you should run your finger around the tank ball. If a black residue comes off on your hand, it's time to replace it *and* book a manicure, pronto!

Lift up the **tank ball/flapper** and gently scrub the **valve seat** and rim with nylon dish pad (no soap!). Be very gentle; you're not trying to sand it, just clean it. Imagine you are polishing something very precious, which you covet, like the diamond engagement ring your sister-in-law got that's at least two carats bigger than the measly chip you're wearing. (Sorry, we got carried away there. Now is not the time to air dirty laundry.)

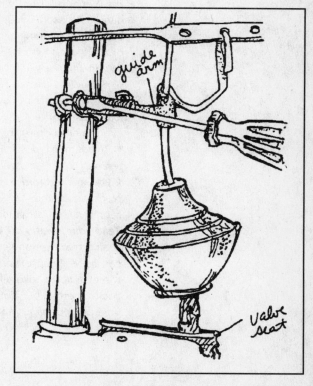

Loosen the screws holding the **guide arm.** Reposition the arm so that it is directly over the hole. If the old tank ball/flapper is not in good condition, remove it and attach a new one. Retighten the screw on the guide arm and check to make sure the ball/flapper falls directly over the hole, sealing it. Turn the water back on and flush the toilet to make sure it's working.

Tip #5: You Know I Can't Hear You When the Water's Running . . . Ooops . . . Bathroom Safety

1. No doubt you've seen this one on an episode of *Murder, She Wrote:*

    The body of a pretty young thing is found dead in a bathroom with no sign of a murder weapon, anywhere. All she has in her lily white hand is a scrub brush, a bottle of ammonia, and a four-carat marquis-cut diamond ring inscribed "To Pumpkin, with love, Harold." How did she die?

    Well, it turns out that the wicked first wife, angered by her rich industrialist ex-husband's second marriage to a much younger, prettier, and oh-so-chirpy bimbette, decided that revenge was her only recourse. So, knowing that despite the bimbette's newfound wealth, she hadn't yet overcome her humble roots and still had a thing about cleaning her own bathrooms, the vengeful first wife had snuck into the bathroom and dumped bleach down the toilet. When wife #2 came in and added her ammonia cleaner down the toilet, the resulting mix of the bleach with the ammonia caused a lethal gas to be emitted which overcame wife #2 and killed her.

    So, unless there is a young second wife somewhere you'd like to bump off or you have a hankering to be seen on *America's Most Wanted,* please **don't mix bleach with ammonia.** Don't even think about using them at the same time.

    Incidentally, Jessica got the first wife to confess by pretending to be a masseuse and kneading it out of her.

2. ***If you spill water into an electric socket, don't try to dry it out*** by plugging in your blow dryer in the same place. (We have all seen the Godfather movies, haven't we?)

3. ***Take your jewelry off before you work.*** It's not dangerous, but seeing that diamond earring drop make its way down the drain can be really upsetting. Of course the accident might give you the chance to take all your pipes apart and see how they fit back together, but if it's come to this, you have way too much time on your hands and should consider getting a hobby.

4. While we're on the subject of chemicals, **_don't store anything that can react with water under your sink._** By this we mean Drano, acids, and so on. If you're like us, you probably keep your cleaning products under your sink. Half a cup of water in a can of Drano and BOOM, you can have an explosion. So check your labels and move anything that says "Do not mix with water" to a cool, dry place.

Tip #6: Oh, What a Little Makeup Can Do!

1. Sometimes, after you have finished doing some bathroom repairs or just after normal wear and tear, you will notice little chips in the porcelain on your tub, toilet, or sink. These are very easy to fix and should be taken care of as the need arises. Apply a **_porcelain enamel repairer_** with a small paintbrush (the kind your kid uses to paint model airplanes will work just fine). **_Blend_** the edges of the paint lightly, extending out and feathering from the chip to the edge of the enamel.

2. If you find a **_crack_** in your toilet tank, take care of it at once so you don't have a major leak on your hands. Empty the tank first, and then make sure it is totally dry before you proceed.

   You will need to use a two-part epoxy glue to do the repair, not the fast-setting or instant type glue. The directions on the package will tell you how to mix it, and you can apply it with a fine piece of wood or a toothpick. Wipe away anything that has oozed over and let the whole thing sit overnight before you attempt to paint over it.

   Cover up the crack with an appliance touch-up paint (they come in every color imaginable), wait for it to dry, then, if necessary, use the enamel repairer on top.

TO CAULK OR NOT TO CAULK . . .

Gravity sucks! As is true with all of us, over the years, what was once up, will come down. Thus, your house will start to settle downward with the passage of time and, when it does it'll take your bathtub along with it, causing a slight separation to appear between it and the wall. These and any cracks you might see around the sink or in the shower should be patched up by *recaulking*. This can be accomplished easily with a tube of caulking compound you can buy in any hardware store. (Although they are almost always waterproof, check carefully just to make sure.)

1. *Dry* the area you are going to work on and, if necessary, dig out any old caulk that is loose. (A putty or spackling knife is the best thing to use here.)
2. *Hold* the tube of caulk at an angle to your crack and squeeze out enough to leave a thin line behind as you move along the length of the crack. Keep *squeezing and pushing* the caulk under the crack line as you move down it.
3. When you reach the end, *push* any excess up into the crack, *clean* off the line, and *let set* thoroughly.
4. Wait until it is all hard and dry before you use the tub again.

A WOMAN'S PLACE IS IN THE . . .
KITCHEN REPAIRS

We love our kitchens and bet that most of you do, too. Jeni is an ace baker and has been known to throw together the most amazing concoctions at the drop of a hat. She is also the only known woman to have single-handedly baked her own ten-layer wedding cake on the day of her wedding. ("The best thing about the entire marriage," she just added.)

In any case, we spend a lot of time in the kitchen, and there is nothing worse than being in the middle of preparing some fabulous chocolate mousse or a *très incroyable* coq au vin when your disposal erupts or your dishwasher decides it needs a vacation.

If anything happens with your faucets or your drain, all of the bathroom sink stuff applies here, too, but if **the garbage disposal** or **the dishwasher** goes on the blink, there are a few things you should try before you call for help. Do not, we repeat do not, however, attempt to take the sucker apart by yourself. Not only will you not know what to do, but any damage you cause may conflict with your warranty.

Garbage Disposals

The garbage disposal is the one item in your house that we guarantee will break down at least once a year. Most of the time the damage isn't heavy duty, just a case of something getting caught that you can un-catch.

The first thing you need to do is make sure the switch is off. We know that this sounds elementary, but emergency rooms are full of people who didn't heed this simple caveat. Now, you can very carefully feel around to see if a spoon, piece of glass, or other object has accidentally fallen in. If you find something, remove it. Then proceed as follows:

Try the reset button. There is an interesting feature located along the bottom of your garbage disposal called the reset button. It is sometimes difficult to find so you'll have to get on your hands and knees, reach your hand under the contraption, and feel around until you hit pay dirt. If this sounds a little like the instructions for finding the elusive "G" spot, it is but, trust us, this one really works.

Try turning the disposal back on. If nothing happens, the circuit breaker/fuse might have tripped. (By the way, knowing where your fuse box is is one of those essential things you really must know. It's kind of like knowing that football games are played on Sunday afternoons and Monday nights from September until January. It might not seem important at the time, but it'll come in mighty handy if you need to know which night would *not* be good for your new beau to meet your mother.) Check the fuse box, but don't forget to turn the switch OFF before you do so or you might return to the kitchen only to hear a most unattractive, grinding sound coming from the bowels of your sink. If everything seems fine but it still won't go back on, the blades may be locked.

Shake a broomstick: If the blades are locked, stick a broomstick into the disposal. Notice we said stick, not jam! The purpose of this is to try to loosen up the blades and get them moving again. Wriggle the broom back and forth and try unlocking the blades by pushing against them with the handle. (No cries of "Double, double, toil and trouble" should be allowed from the peanut gallery.)

CAUTION: Make sure the switch is *turned off*. Routinely, no matter how many times we've checked, we double-check before sticking anything down there. A finger is a terrible thing to waste.

If these tricks don't work, you might have burned out the motor and that will require professional help. We'd advise that you call in help before the water backs up in your sink and the lovely smell of garbage invades your kitchen. If that happens, *you* will be the one needing the professional help, not just the sink.

Dishwashers

Recently, Joan's dishwasher seemed to be failing in its duty. Dishes were emerging with all the gunky bits still intact and, on top of that, hard little pellets of soap were spattered everywhere, and a lovely stream of water was pouring forth which the cats all walked in and then tracked across her brand-new blue rug. A plumber was summoned and the cats were banished to the bedroom! After only eight minutes, he announced that he had discovered the problem. We sighed with relief, clapped our hands with glee and expectantly awaited his proclamation. (It had been a *really* slow day.) "The water isn't hot enough," he ruled. Then, with a smile he handed Joan the bill and vanished, leaving Joan to mop up the water by herself. The total damage for these five words of wisdom was $75, approximately the sale cost of those new shoes you've had your eye on.

What's the moral of this story? you may ask. ***Dishwasher detergents need a temperature of 140 degrees F in order to dissolve.*** So if you're having this problem, check the temperature on your hot water heater, and/or switch to a liquid detergent. P.S.: Always keep smelling salts in a handy location. Joan came around nicely after only a few minutes.

Tip #8: Dishwasher Etiquette

If you are having a new dishwasher installed, make sure the drain line from the dishwasher is run into an air stop, not directly into the drain. This is very important, because when there is a backup in the sink or in the garbage disposal, contaminated water will flow backwards into your dishwasher. Not a pretty sight. The air stop prevents this.

The air stop, by the way, is that weird hole next to your faucet that seems to have a cap with holes in it over it. You may have seen water come out of it and wondered where the hell it was coming from. Well, now you know. By the way, if you don't have one, don't let the installer of your next dishwasher get away without putting one in. With the prices they charge, it's the least they can do. Give the guy a glass of iced tea for his trouble and you can call it even.

Washers and Dryers

Once more, these appliances should be left to the pros, but there is one thing that you should remember if you need to use an extension cord for these appliances to reach an outlet. The little ones you use to connect your VCR, TV, and blow dryer are simply not gonna cut it and will, eventually, cause your machine to burn out. You need to get a heavy-duty extension cord that is at least 15 amps.

Also, don't overlook those extended service contracts for your appliances. They cost about fifty bucks a year, but if something major happens, they are worth their weight in gold.

Oh, and if the washer is filling more slowly than usual, check the screens that filter your water. These are on the hoses behind your machine and come off easily.

HOME IMPROVEMENTS (SORRY, WE COULDN'T RESIST)

Now for some of the fun stuff. In addition to using all these practical skills to save time and money, you can now put all of what you have just learned to great use by going shopping! There, now we've gotten your attention. What we had in mind was buying and installing some things that can help you personalize your home.

Unless you are living in a multimillion-dollar, professionally decorated home (and, if you are, you've done pretty damn well for yourself so we're not sure what you are doing reading this book), you probably live in an apartment, condo, or fixer-upper, all of which contain the same old boring chrome fixtures you can find anywhere. Well, you're not boring, so why should your fixtures be? What you must do is take yourself down to any home improvement store and discover a world that, heretofore, has only been known to those in the trade. Why, those sneaky builders were holding out on you! In these vast spaces you will find row upon row of chrome, brass, porcelain, and wood items that you can screw and attach to your heart's content. There are also stores that specialize in selling antique hardware items so you can make your bedroom look just like the one your grandmother used to have. In this section, we will teach you how to change and upgrade the following:

Faucets and knobs
Handles
Showerheads (including those fun massage kinds)
Toilet seats
Toilet paper and towel racks
Medicine cabinets

Future chapters will deal with adding decorative shelves and tile changes.

All really big jobs like installing vanities, changing sinks, and hanging shower doors are things that you should probably leave to professionals. You can do all the choosing, however.

WARNING: These kinds of changes can be addictive. We heard of one woman who developed such a "jones" for chrome and white enamel fixtures that her husband begged her to go back to Charles Jourdan and buy a few more pairs of shoes. Come to think of it, that sounds like a good plan to us!

Change Partners and Dance (Step-by-Step Directions for Swapping Faucets)

Yes, you really do have to turn off the water here, too.

Faucets are connected to the hot and cold supply pipes by *risers*. Undo the **coupling nuts** at each end of the riser and pull the riser out. Set it aside. If you look up under the sink where the buttons of the faucets are, you will see they are held in place by a nut. Undo the **nut**, remove the **washer**, and set it aside. You can now lift out the entire faucet assembly.

Tip #9: De-Puttying

If the putty around the base of the faucet is old, it may be stuck. Try loosening it with the flat blade of a screwdriver. If you don't intend to recycle the faucet, you can tap it gently with a hammer. Be careful not to scratch the sink.

Now that you have the faucet out, you need to thoroughly clean the top of the sink. (You certainly don't want to put your shiny new faucet into an area smeared with the residue of last week's spaghetti dinner.) Any old putty or caulk should be removed, as well as the gunk. This is not only important cosmetically but, in case your new faucet has a slightly smaller base, it will prevent leaks.

Apply **plumber's putty** to the bottom of the new faucet. This is much easier than caulking—think Play-Doh. Take a lump of putty and roll it around in your hands until it's pliable. Then roll it out into a long snake, about a quarter inch thick. Press this into the underside of the new faucet and around the holes in the sink. If you have any left, you can make believe it's cookie dough and cook up some little snacks for the "lovely" little kiddies next door who like to ring your doorbell and then run away before you can answer it. That should put them out of commission for a little while—or at least until their second set of teeth comes in.

Position the faucet over the sink, making sure that the new **risers** and **drain stop** are aligned with the old holes. Press into place firmly, rocking back and forth slightly to spread the putty.

Back under the sink, attach the **mounting screws,** then screw the **washers** and **nuts** onto the **risers.** Then, using two wrenches, connect the risers to the faucet and to the water supply. Hold the riser with one wrench, tighten the nut with the other.

By the way, we originally felt that most plumbers were rather dull and humorless fellows. Then we found out that they have a new name for the little washers and nuts that attach the mounting screws onto the risers. They call them **pro-hookers.** That piece of information made us wonder what plumbers are *really* doing between the time they said they would show up to fix the leak in the faucet and the time they actually do.

The last thing you need to do is to flush the lines. This will get rid of any debris and will set the seals. Remove the **aerator** at the spout and let the water run a couple of minutes. Screw the aerator back on and stand back to admire your gorgeous new faucet.

Replacing Knobs and Handles

Joan has recently gone knob crazy. She started out in the kitchen and has now refitted every single doorknob and cabinet pull in her house. Having learned from our mistakes, we have a few tips to offer.

1. Knobs, like sinks, come in all sizes and shapes. Be aware that if you are changing from a single screw to one that has two, or vice versa, you will have to drill new holes and the old ones might show. Also, if you are replacing a handle that has two screws with another, the distance between the screws may be different. Unless you have your

heart set on something that doesn't match, it's much easier to plop a new one into the same place as the old.

2. If you are replacing the knobs on two drawers that are in a corner at right angles to each other, make sure that when you pull one drawer out, it will clear the new knob on the other.

3. If you get fancy and decide to put a knob or handle where none existed before, this will require drilling holes. Please, please (we cannot emphasize this enough) measure carefully and make sure that the size of the drill bit you use is right for the size of the screw that goes with the knob or handle you have chosen. One look at the lopsided handles in Joan's kitchen and you will understand the wisdom of our advice. Let's put it this way, picture the bodies on the field after the Battle of Gettysburg and you might have a sense of the damage she inflicted.

4. Doorknobs are a total trip. They can alter the whole mood of any bathroom and, if you change your fixtures from brass to chrome, say, make sure that the integrity of your decor remains intact. (God forbid, you didn't match.) The directions on the packages really explain it all for you, but there are a couple of things to watch out for.

   A lock consists of four parts: the **latch bolt,** the **exterior assembly,** the **interior assembly,** and the **strike.** The latch bolt is the item that goes through the middle of the door. The exterior assembly is the one used on the side of the door from which you enter, and the interior assembly is on the other side. The strike is the small metal frame that fits in the doorjamb.

   a. You will have to remove the old lock by, first, unscrewing the old latch bolt and then unscrewing the screw from the exterior assembly which holds it all in place. Before you start, check to see if the screws used to hold it all together were Phillips or flat head and then use the appropriate screwdriver.

   b. Put the new latch bolt in place and screw it in.

   c. Press the latch bolt in and then push the spindles and stems of the new interior assembly through the latch.

d. Place the exterior assembly on the door, align screw holes with stems of both assemblies, insert screws, and tighten.

e. If necessary, remove the old strike by unscrewing it and then replace it with the new one. Be careful that you place it so the curved side is facing down. If you don't, the door will not close tightly in the latch.

f. Always keep the little unlocking device that comes with the lock in a safe place *outside* of the room in case you lock yourself out. (You can guess how Joan came up with this tip, can't you?)

g. Make sure that the lock set you buy will sufficiently cover the hole that already exists in the door. If you are buying antique doorknobs, it will probably be necessary to mount a plate over the hole before you do the knob. That's okay since period brass and pewter plates can really add a distinctive look to any room.

Please forgive Joan's enthusiasm for this topic, but changing doorknobs is the one thing that Joan can do that Jeni can't, so she kind of wanted to show off for you a little. What? Oh, yeah . . . Jeni just made a crack about how Joan once locked herself in a room by putting the *interior* assembly on the *outside* by mistake and then forgetting to unlock the little doohickey in the handle first. She had to climb out onto her balcony and around the other side in order to get back in. I guess that's what you get for being too cocky about something, huh?

5. You can put in some really fun and distinctive knobs and handles if you hunt out salvage places, stores that specialize in antique hardware, or order through catalogues. A shiny Bakelite handle from the forties or a faceted glass knob from the twenties can really make your bathroom or kitchen unique.

Installing New Showerheads

Most new showerheads are remarkably easy to install. You simply unscrew the old one, retape the threads, and screw the new one in. Low-flow showerheads have come a long way; gone is the miserable trickle of the past. You can now find low-flow heads with massagers, antiscald devices, and so on. We are particularly fond of the massagers. After a hard day, there is nothing like the soothing pulse of water on all your tension areas. You'll feel like you're in a spa. Speaking of antiscald devices, if you have children, you should seriously consider installing these. They screw right onto the faucet in place of the aerator and can prevent nasty burns.

Tip #10: Forewarned Is Forearmed

If you need to change the shower arm, don't use pliers to move it; you could easily damage it. Instead, take a screwdriver and insert it into the hollow arm. Hold the end of the screwdriver and using it as leverage, move the arm that way. The reason to do it this way is that because the tube is hollow, it's easily bent. The screwdriver re-enforces the tube from the inside.

Replacing Toilet Seats

This is an easy way to spiff things up. These days, toilet seats come in several different sizes and shapes and colors. We've never acquired a taste for the padded ones, but we do understand their appeal.

The best thing to do is to take the old one with you so you can match it. All you have to do is unscrew the bolts on either side of the seat. Most modern seats use plastic or nylon nuts and bolts, but if you have an old one with rusty metal bolts, use WD 40 or any kind of penetrating oil to remove the bolts. As a last resort, you might have to cut them off with a hacksaw, but this is rare. If it comes to this and you decide to go ahead, remember to protect the surface of the bowl from scratches with tape or fabric.

Changing Toilet-Paper and Towel Holders

Unless yours are ceramic and built into the wall, holders are easy to change. Sometimes they even fall off all by themselves due to either faulty installation or the fact that they hold one of the most used items in the house. However, despite the huge variety of choices of styles and materials, you will be pleased to know that they are almost always mounted in the same way.

First, you have to unscrew the one that is in place now. You will find a setscrew at the base of the fixture. Once it is off, you will find that, behind it, there is a plate attached to the wall with screws. This is designed to be hidden by the rack itself when it is hung from it. Be careful here: common sense will tell you that the plate should be hung with the "cupped" side facing the wall. *Au contraire!* The flat side should be against the wall with the side that has the little ridges facing out. If you don't get it right, you will not be able to attach the setscrew that goes under the rod to secure the mounting and it will come off with the first good rotation of the roll.

If you aren't moving the fixture and can reuse the old plate, you've lucked out. Otherwise, determine where you want the rack to go, measure, double-check your measurements, then drill away.

Tip #11: Being on the Level: Measuring

In order to make sure your rack is level, drill the holes for one of the wall plates only, then mount it. Put the other wall plate where you think it should go, then use a carpenter's level to check it. This will save you a lot of aggravation when you realize you have to take the thing back off the wall, redrill, AND patch and repaint the holes you just put in the wrong place.

Also, after the holes for the plate screws are drilled, make sure that you use anchors to hold the screws in place. Unless you are drilling directly into wood, screws alone will not hold up. Remember to use the right-sized drill bit for your screw or anchor. (More on drilling and anchors in a later chapter.)

All toilet-paper holders, towel racks, and soap dishes are hung in exactly the same way, so if you do one, you can do them all. And we have.

Installing a New Medicine Cabinet

Most old cabinets were designed to fit between the wall studs and are small by today's standards. We guess that in the olden days, before there were all those skin enhancement products with an alphabet soup of ingredients for keeping us young and beautiful, there wasn't as much need for space as there is now. Actually, between the two of us, we need four shelves just for our under-eye depuffers, over-eye moisturizers, and all 'round line removers, and that's not even counting night creams, day creams, throat creams, and bust-firming gels. We guess you could say that we are two women always on a quest for space.

Provided you are replacing your old recessed cabinet with a similarly sized new one, this is easy to do. If, however, you long for bright lights, lots of shelves, new mirrors, and more space (something roughly three times what you've got now), consider some alternatives. Perhaps more than one cabinet is in order—if you've ruled out getting rid of all your jars and just getting plastic surgery. If you have extra wall space, you could hang matching cabinets on opposite walls. If not, you could opt for a surface-mounted, rather than recessed cabinet.

If you plan on putting a new cabinet into the same space, before you do anything else, you should check to make sure you can find a new one that will fit. Measure the size of the *wall opening*, not the cabinet, carefully. On cabinets, this is listed as the "raw space" measurement. If nothing fits, consider placing a surface-mounted cabinet over the space.

STEP BY STEP

If you look inside the old cabinet, you will see screws on both sides going into the wall. Remove these, then pull the cabinet out. If it seems stuck, check on the outside where it meets the wall; years of paint may have accumulated, causing it to stick. Try breaking the seal with a utility knife or flat screwdriver. Be careful if you use the screwdriver as leverage since you can damage the wall.

Once you've removed the old cabinet, all you have to do is slide the similarly sized new one in its place and bolt it to the wall.

If your choice is a surface-mounted cabinet, make sure it completely covers the hole in the wall. Surface-mounted cabinets are attached to the wall studs at the back, not on the sides. These all have instructions, but there are a couple tips we'd like to offer. The cabinet should hang about eight inches above the back of the sink. Use a carpenter's level to make sure your holes are level and definitely use anchors.

There. Now that you have all that extra space, take this opportunity to go through your old makeup jars and bottles and throw out the ones you haven't used in a long time. If you have a lipstick called "Spring Prom," an eye shadow that's robin's egg blue, or a tube of Clearasil, you are definitely overdue for some spring cleaning.

AN OUNCE OF PREVENTION, OR CREATING A MAINTENANCE CHECKLIST

We've all heard the expression "Nothing lasts forever." Well, alas, it's true. And that goes for home repairs, especially. If something wore out or broke once, there is a good chance that it just might do it again if you don't take care of it.

Here is a list of things you should maintain on a regular basis in your bathroom and kitchen and a recap of how often you need to tend to them.

BATHROOM	HOW OFTEN
Clean **drain stoppers** of gunk and hair.	Every two months
Put a tablespoon of cooking or mineral oil down the **drain**.	Once a month
Remove **sink** aerator and soak overnight in de-scaling solution.	Every two months

KITCHEN	HOW OFTEN
Pour a tablespoonful of any cooking oil down the drain of the **garbage disposal**. This will help lubricate the parts.	Every month
Scrub the **dishwasher** with vinegar or other solvent to remove mineral deposits. Pay particular attention to arm, filter screen, pump cover, and drain area.	Every six months
Dust and clean your **refrigerator coils**. This helps it run efficiently and saves you money.	Every six months
Remove and clean the filters on the water lines of your **washing machine**.	Every three months
Remove **sink** aerator and sprayer attachment, soak overnight in vinegar or solvent de-scaling solution.	Every two months

Water Heaters

You should flush these out **twice a year**. This is easy to do; just attach a hose to the faucet at the bottom of the heater. Run the end of the hose to a drain, then open the faucet. The water in the tank will flush out through the hose, taking with it all the sediment that has accumulated. When it's clear, close the faucet and remove the hose. The tank will refill just as it always does.

TAKE FIVE

Okay, ladies, are you still with us? Well, we have some good news: the plumbing is, by far, the worst of the deal and you survived just fine. Now that you have done some of the messiest jobs around the house, onward to some of the other areas. Come on now, put out that cigarette and get to work! There are bolts to tighten and sockets to be plugged all over the place.

5

If Gypsy Rose Lee Could Do It

STRIPPING, SPACKLING, AND PAINTING

You know that time of the month when you have that insatiable urge to book a trip to Paris or buy a complete Donna Karan ensemble *before* it goes on sale or chop five inches off the hair you've been growing out since the last time you got the urge to cut it? So, what do you end up doing? You buy a new tube of lipstick, of course. Well, the rooms in your house get those urges, too, but they choose to tell you of their anxiety by letting little cracks appear in the walls or by starting to peel their outer layers, or by just screaming at you, "Can't you think of anything more original than Navajo White?" When you feel that the walls of your house are trying to tell you something, you have two choices: renew your prescription for Prozac or make a trip down to your local paint store.

In this chapter we will show you how to give your walls the equivalent of a Lancôme makeover that can entail as little as an afternoon of patching and fixing to as much as a full-scale repainting. You'll be amazed at how much better your environment will look when you get rid of those nasty little holes in the wall where the pictures of your ex and his lovely family once hung. Did the moving men leave an unsightly blemish when your new armoire had a head-on collision with the dining room wall? Have no fear; you can take care of that, too. And, if the blinding whiteness of your walls has made you feel like yelling "Mush!" to your bichon frise, just adding a little color to your woodwork and door trims can bring you in from the cold. Of course, for the really ambitious, we will give you a "how to" on the E-ticket ride of painting: repainting an entire room without the aid of a net.

We will look at this important and fun (well, it can be) topic with an eye to three main areas: *STRIPPING, SPACKLING, and PAINTING.*

STRIPPING PAINT, WOODWORK, WALLPAPER

Jeni learned the three P's of successful painting from her mother: *Preparation, Patience,* and *Persnicketiness.* When Jeni was a wee thing, she and her sister lived in an apartment with ornate plaster moldings and high ceilings in every room. You know the type: just picture the apartment in *Rosemary's Baby.* Well, let's take the devil imagery one step further. Jeni's mother asked her and her sister to paint their bedroom, and after many

days of backbreaking labor, they were finally finished. As they lay exhausted on the floor, admiring the results of their efforts, they suddenly heard the door slam and then felt the floorboards creak beneath them. Their mother had entered the room! As she loomed over their prostrate bodies they looked up to see that she had come armed with teeny, tiny art brushes, one in each hand, pointed straight at them. She then advised her children that they were not yet finished and that they now had to go back over their work to check for any little pinholes that might have eluded their attention on the first go-around.

Well, while we don't advocate that kind of preoccupation with detail, preparing your surface before painting by ridding it of anything that might mar it is a good idea—either that or go find a kid of your own whom you can bully around.

That having been said, the first thing to do is make sure that the surface you are going to paint is clean and smooth. While you can paint over a coat or two of old paint on a dry wall, you'll want to remove *multiple* layers of old paint on woodwork. Getting rid of loose wallpaper is a must if you're planning on replacing it with paint.

Paint can be removed from woodwork either by **chemical solvents, sanding**, or with a **heat gun**. The choice depends on several things:

1. How much surface there is and how detailed it is
2. Cost
3. Ease of application
4. Whether or not you are willing to work with hazardous chemicals

If your woodwork surface is very detailed, as it can often be in older houses, sanding the paint off might remove some of the detail, so chemical solvents are the best way to go.

Sanding

If you are removing paint from woodwork by sanding, you should start out with an *electric sander*. These can easily be rented, should you not wish to buy one. Electric sanders send stuff flying everywhere, so wear a dust mask and close off the rest of the house by shutting a door where possible or by hanging sheets of plastic over open areas. You should also consider safety goggles or glasses as the accessories needed to complete your ensemble.

NOTE: If you want a fine finish, if the wood is heavily detailed, or if access to a machine is difficult, you will need to follow with sandpaper or steel wool.

For our purposes, there are three basic types of electric sanders: *orbital*, *random orbital*, and *belt*. They vary according to the way in which the abrasive surface moves. We are going to describe them all, but in our opinion, the only one worth having is the *random orbital* sander.

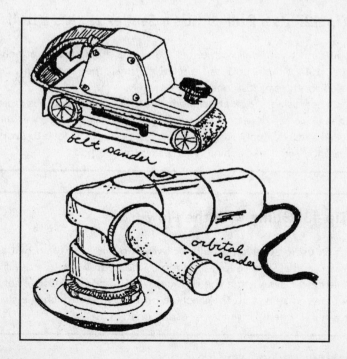

ORBITAL SANDERS

This type moves the sanding paper in a small circular or oval pattern. *Orbitals* can be difficult to use without leaving circular tracks behind.

BELT SANDERS

Belt sanders do the job by using a continuously rotating loop of sandpaper. Be warned: the really enormous, heavy ones are quite difficult to operate and often leave big gouges in the surface in their wake.

RANDOM ORBITAL SANDERS

Our favorite type of sander moves the paper in an overall, but loosely circular, pattern. The *random orbital sanders* are designed to prevent marks and are the best and easiest to use. They are also versatile and can accomplish just about anything you might have to do.

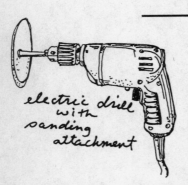

electric drill with sanding attachment

Tip #2: It's a Drill . . . It's a Sander . . . It's a Drill

You can fit your drill with either a disk or a drum sanding attachment. Since their surfaces are relatively small, they should only be used for the smallest jobs.

When using a **disk attachment,** tilt it about ten degrees from the surface and use only the top half of the disk. (The center will leave a mark.) Apply pressure lightly, as it can be difficult to avoid leaving swirl marks behind when using this method.

Tip #3: Going with the Flow

When using an electric sander, always go with the grain of the wood and always keep it in motion. When you want to stop, lift the sander away from the surface, THEN turn it off. Conversely, when you start, turn the machine on *before* you touch the surface, not when the sander is resting on it.

So you've got your sander in one hand and you are ready to load sandpaper onto it. Now, we heard that rumbling out there—you're asking, "What *is* sandpaper exactly?" Well, despite its name, it isn't sand and it isn't necessarily paper, either. It's an abrasive attached to a composition material. As you sand, the crystals that make up the abrasive break down, exposing new, sharp surfaces. There is a dizzying variety of "sandpapers," which are made up of every kind of abrasive from flint to silicon carbide to aluminum oxide. However, the selection isn't that mysterious, as they are designed for different surfaces and are, surprise surprise, conveniently labeled "For wood," "For metal," "For plastic," etc. Boy, were we ever pleased to find this example of a woman's touch in such an, otherwise, male bastion.

To further clarify things, below you will find an overview of the type of sandpaper you will need for each of the different surfaces you might face.

Types of Sandpaper

SURFACE	FEATURES
Garnet	Commonly used for hand sanding on wood. Soft, won't burn wood if used with a power sander, but not good for metal.
Emery	Very hard surface, good for metal but not wood, as crystals dull instead of breaking to give new edges. Use with an oil lubricant on surface and a power sander.
Crocus	Softer than emery, good for polishing metal lightly, power and hand sanding.
Aluminum oxide	Very common and good for both wood and metal, power and hand sanding.
Coated aluminum oxide	A new product, the coating sloughs off while sanding, taking the debris with it and preventing clogging between the crystals. Good for polyurethane and water-based finishes. Best used with a power sander.

SURFACE	FEATURES
Silicon carbide	Will give a smoother surface on wood than aluminum oxide. Lubricate with water or oil to prevent clogging up. Can also be used on nonferrous metal.
Ceramic aluminum oxide	*The* choice for professional floor sanders, since it wears out more slowly than other materials. It is especially good for power sanding wood and metal.

When you have decided on the surface of the sandpaper you are going to use, the next choice you will have to make concerns the sandpaper's **grade**. Sandpaper comes in grades ranging from extracoarse to ultrafine. Each grade will also have a "grit" number on it, something like "100" or "200" that will refer to the number of openings per square inch in a screen that the crystals were able to pass through before being attached to the paper. The rule of thumb is, the higher the number, the finer the sandpaper. Generally speaking, start out with coarse and work your way to fine. You will get the best results if you step down without skipping grades. Although you will get a finer surface by sanding rather than just stripping, be warned—sanding takes a *lot* of patience and elbow grease. By the way, whatever you leave in the crevices is still going to be there when you paint, so make sure you clean out the leftover dust, thoroughly, before you paint.

After you have removed most of the paint or finish with the machine, you will be ready to move on to hand sanding. By the way, the heavier the paper backing is, the faster you will be able to sand, so if the paper is thin, try wrapping it around a block of wood or other hard surface for added backing. For further information on sanding, see our chapter on refinishing furniture.

Tip #4: On the Cutting Edge

Don't cut sandpaper with your scissors, as the abrasion on the paper will make them very dull, very quickly. Instead, score the back of the paper with a **utility knife**, fold it along the crease several times, and then tear it.

Chemical Strippers

All strippers contain dangerous chemicals and should be used with care. Follow the manufacturer's directions, wear gloves and protective eyewear, and ventilate, ventilate, ventilate. If you are working near a gas appliance (stove, heater, etc.), turn the gas off so that the pilot is out. Don't smoke. Not only is lighting a match *not* a good idea, but some solvents give off fumes that, upon inhalation with cigarette smoke, can be toxic.

Tip #5: Putting on a New Face

If you find that your beautiful, newly painted room is marred by the old door which is, easily, wearing seventeen coats of old paint ranging in hues from persimmon to marigold, relax—there are people who get paid big bucks to strip it for you. Most will pick up and rehang the door for you—for a small fee, of course.

Be warned: There are two types of commercial stripping processes, *hot* and *cold*.

The *hot* process can damage the wood and will definitely raise the grain on the wood. You will either need to sand it yourself, afterwards, or have them do it. The *cold* process is more expensive but requires less finishing afterwards.

Although it is always necessary to read the individual manufacturer's directions before you use any stripper, we will outline below the basic steps for each type of chemical stripper.

GELS OR LIQUIDS (THESE CONTAIN METHYLENE CHLORIDE.)

1. After covering the surrounding area for protection, apply a coat of stripper to the wood, making sure it gets into all the crevices.
2. Wait ten to thirty minutes, then check to see if the paint will lift easily by scraping off a small area. It's a lot of work to scrape the wood, so if the stripper hasn't worked its way down to the last layer of paint, add more and check again after a few minutes.
3. Once it is ready, scrape away. You can use a tool called a **shavehook** to get in the crevices. You can also use **steel wool** dipped in stripper to get the last bits. As with cotton balls and nail polish remover, you need to keep using a fresh area so you don't redeposit the paint as you scrub.
4. After stripping, rinse the area with water or with turpentine before you start to paint. If you use water, be careful not to soak the wood as this will raise the grain and can damage it.

Tip #6: Save an Oak

If you're stripping oak, don't use steel wool or other metals; they can react with the wood and leave stains.

PASTES (THESE CONTAIN A CAUSTIC AGENT.)

1. Spread the paste on the surface.
2. To prevent it from drying out while it works, cover the surface with a polyethylene sheet or material provided by the manufacturer.
3. Check it after the recommended time, usually several hours. If it has become too dry, you can soften it with water. Peel it off when it's ready.
4. Rinse the wood and let dry before refinishing.

Heat Guns

Heat guns look like heavy-duty blow-dryers for those really *bad* hair days and, while they are fast and efficient, if they are not used with care, they can scorch the wood, your designer working togs, and you, in the process. The electric guns are easier to control than the gas ones and can be equipped with several different nozzles to focus the heat in different patterns.

Basically, you hold the heat gun about two inches from the wood, sweep it over a small area, a little bit at a time, and, as the paint bubbles up, follow with a scraper.

CAUTION: Don't be a ninny and test the gun by putting your hand in front of it. Paint will bubble up in a matter of seconds, so you can imagine what it would do to your skin. Also, be very careful if you are using a heat gun on the paint around windows as it can crack the glass if you use too much heat.

Tip #7: Pace Yourself

Stripping wood is a very time-consuming process, whatever method you use. Take frequent breaks as you work or you might get discouraged, rush the process, or quit.

It's better to finish an area completely and be happy with the results than to plow on like a maniac only to run out of steam halfway through when you realize how much more you have to do. Joan has a friend whose living room looks like something Van Gogh might have created after sipping a little too much of that absinthe he liked so much. See, she started stripping paint on a whim and then decided she'd had enough and stopped. Of course the fact that she started the job on the day her husband came home with a brand-new foosball table and stopped the day he got rid of it *might* have something to do with it. You can be the judge.

Stripping Wallpaper

If your wallpaper isn't torn or peeling off and if it isn't from the seventies (i.e., Mylared or velvet flocked as were most wallpapers from that tasteful decade), you can prime it and paint right over it. If, however, you want to remove it, there are a few simple steps you need to follow:

1. Use either a sponge and spray bottle or rent a commercial steamer and then **soak** the wallpaper with warm water and a little detergent or stripping powder.

   NOTE: If the paper is the "washable" type, you will need to **score** it first so that the water can penetrate.

Tip #8: How Dry I Am

Work on only the area you can reasonably expect to scrape before it dries, otherwise you'll just have to keep rewetting the paper. The rate of speed at which people work varies from person to person and room to room, but calm down. To our knowledge, wallpaper wetting is not, yet, an Olympic event.

---

2. After about twenty minutes, **test** to see if the paper is ready to be peeled off. Take a wide scraper and start at a seam, carefully lifting the paper up. It should come off fairly easily so, if it doesn't, rewet and try again in a few minutes. Be careful not to soak the wall or to gouge it with the scraper.

Tip #9: How Shocking!

CAUTION: Don't use water around wall outlets or switches, unless you shut down the power first. Be sure the area is completely dry before you turn it back on.

If your walls are covered with vinyl wallpaper, you can probably just peel it off without wetting it down. There is a paper lining behind it that you can paint over or leave on if you're rewallpapering.

THERE'S MORE THERE THAN MEETS THE EYE . . . SPACKLING

If you think that you're now ready to hoist the old paintbrush, think again. See, the trick to a great paint job or, for that matter, even a good one is **preparation**. Now that your surface is, more or less, naked, all those little flaws you've been covering up will be there for all the world to see.

Stand back and take a good look at what you have wrought. If the surface isn't smooth, clean, and free of cracks, holes, or layers of tape from that old Woodstock poster you never bothered to take down, you won't be happy with the results and you'll just have to put that bedraggled poster back up where it was in the first place—and, frankly, dear, Woodstock was a long, *long* time ago.

Let's look at some of the most common blemishes you might find on your wall surface and how to remedy them. Below we have divided them into those types of repairs that are done on **plaster** walls and those that are done on **wallboard** or *Sheetrock*.

Filling in Nail Holes and Small Cracks in Wallboard or Plaster

Materials needed: spackling paste and/or joint compound

Tools needed: putty knife, utility knife, fine sandpaper

These are usually the most obvious faults in your wall and can be handled with relatively little fuss and bother if you follow the steps listed below:

1. *Clean* out any dust or plaster that may be in the hole. You can do this by blowing into the hole, but be careful that it doesn't fly back into your face. This is especially true for contact lens wearers, since little flecks of plaster are not the most comfortable things to have caught underneath your lenses. (A more practical way to do it would be to use a small vacuum nozzle. This would also be good when you want to get dust out of crevices and moldings before you apply your paint later. A small whisk broom will work, too.)

2. Next, **put a small dab** of spackling on your putty knife and **press** it into the hole. (It's a little bit squishy in texture—kind of like Play-Doh without the colors.)

3. Once you have applied enough to sufficiently fill the offending hole or crack, hold the blade of the knife at an angle but make sure you keep the edge flat against the wall. Then, just **brush** it across the hole and you will see all the lumps smooth out. When it looks right to you, **let it dry** for a couple of hours. (You can use the time to write those thank-you notes you've been putting off since Christmas or take a few turns on your exercise bike.)

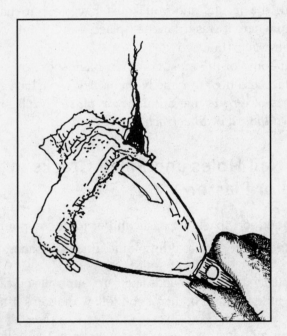

4. Since the material used to fill the hole has a tendency to shrink when it dries, you might need to **apply one more coat** in order to fill the hole completely. Remember to let it dry. When it looks flush with the wall, it's a go.

5. Now, **sand** lightly with fine sandpaper. Don't press into the hole with the paper as if you're attacking a nail that broke off before a

big date; just lightly feather the edges to blend into the wall until the whole surface is smooth to the touch.

While you use the same technique to fill in a small crack as you did for a hole, cracks are persistent little buggers that sometimes, just when you think they're gone forever, simply reappear. Don't curse at them. You've done nothing wrong; that's just the nature of the beast. Go take a piece of **fiberglass mesh drywall tape** (you can find it at any hardware store) and press it over the stubborn crack. Now use a wide putty knife and spread the spackling compound **through** the tape into the crack. Let it dry, sand, and apply another coat. Hopefully the crack will take the hint and stay hidden.

Tip #10: Blending In

The trick to getting spackling to blend in seamlessly is to make each successive layer of the compound wider than the one before. **Brush** over the top of the one underneath and **smooth** out to the edge. The first one may only be two inches wide, but the next should be three or four and the one after that, wider still. Each time, take care to feather it away from the crack to blend with the wall.

Deeper into the Breech, Dear Friends . . . or Repairing Large and Deep Cracks in Plaster

Additional tools: spray bottle for water

Where we live, in the great Southern California land of sun, sand, and earthquakes, we all had a rude shock a few years ago when, after the shaking stopped, we found that our lovely walls were now crisscrossed with earthquake-induced cracks. For that matter, so were our faces. It doesn't take an earthquake to make cracks, however; the simple action of a house settling into its foundation can also make irregular lines appear in your walls. So if you find a crack that is wide in one part and hairline in others, you need to take some steps in addition to the previous procedure.

1. A hairline crack can be deceiving since, in reality, the crack underneath is probably much deeper than what you see on the surface. Grab onto a **utility knife** and dig around the edge of the hairline to make a shallow V. This will make it easier to force the putty into the center of the crack. Be sure that you take time to remove any dust when you are finished.

2. Now comes the **spray bottle** part. Use it to **wet** the crack and area right around it, taking care that it becomes damp, but not soggy. You'll want to make sure that the dry plaster doesn't absorb all the moisture from the compound when it dries since the differences in the texture of the two surfaces can make it crack again.

3. Ready? Now pick up the **putty knife** again and apply the first coat of compound into the crack. Wait a couple of hours and when the stuff is dry, apply the next coat. Continue until the crack is filled and you have blended the top coat into the wall.

There's a Hole in My Bucket . . . Patching Small Holes in Sheetrock

Materials needed: patching plaster, spackling compound, cardboard, string

Tools needed: wide putty knife

Okay, so remember when you got so mad at your ex the time you purchased theater tickets for that totally sold-out play but he went to play poker with that obnoxious guy from his office who always refers to women as "chicks"? And remember how you slammed the door so hard on him that the doorknob got stuck in the wall? Well, the legacy of that incident is the grapefruit-sized hole that has been gracing your bedroom wall ever since. We think that now's the time to get rid of that nasty reminder of such a black hole in your marital communication.

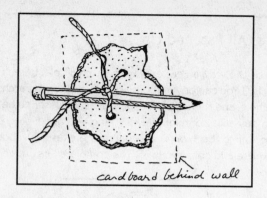

cardboard behind wall

1. **Cut** a piece of cardboard so that it's about half an inch wider than the hole, then punch two holes in it and thread a piece of string through them.
2. Holding the string in one hand, **bend** or **fold** the cardboard so that it will fit through the hole into the wall cavity behind.
3. **Pull** on the string so that the cardboard straightens out and lies flat against the back side of the hole. This way, the putty will have something to set against and you won't have all the putty falling backward into the wall cavity.
4. Follow the manufacturer's directions for **mixing** the patching plaster (probably about a cup should do it), then spread some into the hole with the putty knife, making sure that some of it goes between the cardboard and the wall.
5. When that's done, **pull the string taut** and continue filling the hole until the level is just about an eighth of an inch below the wall. Now you have two options: you can either tie the string to a pencil as shown below, or if you've got nothing better to do, you can hold the string taut for a few minutes while the plaster sets. (For those of you who have a problem with the concept of just "being" for a few minutes—this is where Joan should take note—we guess you *could* use your free hand to return some phone calls. It usually takes only ten minutes to set, so don't call your former college roommate whom you haven't seen in ten years.)
6. When it's done, **cut and remove** the string, score the surface lightly, and finish it off by applying two coats of spackling compound.

Tip #11: All Patched Up

There is, by the way, an easier way to patch a hole. (Aren't we just little devils?) You can buy a fiberglass-and-aluminum patch, place it over the hole, and then apply the plaster as we describe below. You can even buy a kit containing everything you need: patch, plaster, spackling knife, the works. The patches are usually about eight inches square and cost about $5. The complete kits are about $10.

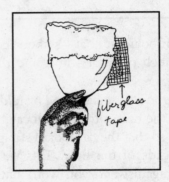

NOTE: Since they are applied *over* the hole, not behind it, it will take a little more work on your part to achieve a smooth finish that is level with the wall. Whichever way you decide to go, the directions below for finishing the surface apply equally.

Did a Spaceship Land There, or What? . . . Filling Major Holes in Plaster

Materials needed: patching plaster

Tools needed: hammer, chisel, putty knife, spray water bottle

The difference between small holes and major ones is in the eye of the beholder. A good rule of thumb, however, is that if you can put your foot through it, it's probably major.

That having been said, if your hole is of the gapingly large variety, by following the handy hints we give you here, you can close that gap, forever.

1. **Remove** all loose plaster so that the patching plaster will adhere well. If there are any cracked pieces that won't come loose easily, place the chisel against the area you are trying to remove and tap it gently with the hammer. Work all the edges of the hole so that there are no more cracks visible; otherwise, the crack will bleed into the new plaster.

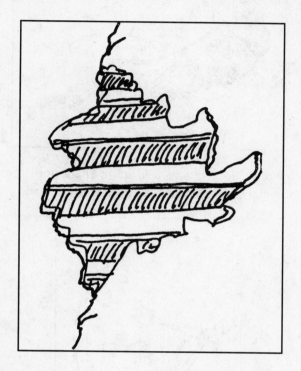

2. Once you can see underneath the plaster, you will find wood strips that are nailed to the wall studs. The strips are called **laths** and are what the plaster adheres to. Any lath that is broken or loose should be replaced or renailed to the stud. (In life, we'd just replace the stud if it was broken or loose, so go figure.)
3. **Wet down** the edges of the hole with water so that they are damp, not soggy as we cautioned earlier.
4. **Mix** up a batch of the patching plaster and apply the first layer. Like frosting a cake, it is more important that you try to cover the whole area in a thin layer than create a deep layer over part of the hole. You can always add more on top.

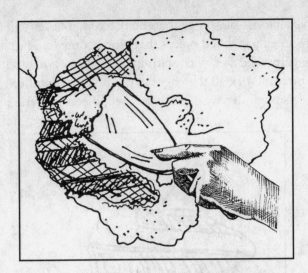

5. Let it *dry* and, if necessary, *add* more coats until the final level is about one-eighth inch below the surrounding wall.

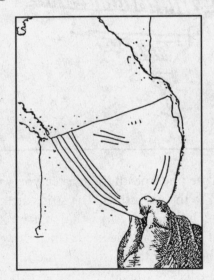

6. When it is completely dry, *score* lightly and *apply* a final coat of patching plaster.

7. For the *finishing* touch, use a wide putty knife to apply a top coat of spackling compound, remembering to feather it out from the hole several inches.

Coming Apart at the Seams . . .
Replacing Loose Drywall Tape

Materials needed: joint compound, fiberglass mesh drywall tape

Tools needed: utility knife, wide putty knife, sandpaper

If your house resembles the "before" of *Mr. Blandings Builds His Dream House,* your walls are probably decorated with confetti-like strands of dry wall tape, dangling in the air. **Drywall tape** is a paper-based tape that is used to cover the seams in sheetrock. Occasionally, air gets trapped under it when the joint compound is applied, causing the tape to bubble up and come loose.

1. **Cut** the loose tape away from the wall. If there is a seam below it, this is where two sheets of drywall are next to each other and you'll need to replace the tape to prevent cracking.

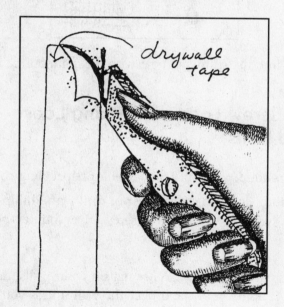

2. Cut a piece of **fiberglass mesh drywall tape** to fit the missing section. This is easier to use than regular drywall tape as it is self-adhesive and prevents the formation of air bubbles that would crack the surface.

3. *Press* it into the seam and coat with the compound.

Having a Screw Loose . . . Fixing Loose Wallboard Nails

Materials needed: drywall screws, joint or spackling compound

Tools needed: cordless screwdriver or drill with Phillips head attachment (you can use a regular screwdriver, but it'll be a lot of work), hammer, nail set

If you're not sure if you have loose nails in your walls, don't try to figure it out by running your hand over the wall unless you're up-to-date with your tetanus shot boosters. Careful visual inspection will do just as well: in other words, they'll be sticking out of the wall.

Just spackling over these won't work since they'll only pop up again when the wall shifts. What you need to do is *secure* the board around the nail so there is no pressure on it. This can best be accomplished by putting a drywall screw about an inch above and below the offending nail. (Try to do this so that the screw is set slightly below the wall surface, but not so deep that you tear the surface paper.)

Because of the importance of the placement of the nail, it is a good idea to use a **nail set** on the loose nail and use it to drive the nail into the wall with a hammer. A nail set, as we told you in the tool chapter, is really a tapered cylinder about three inches long which has an enlarged, easy-to-hit surface for the hammer to come in contact with and a narrow end that you place on the nail head. The nail set will let you push the nail into the wall without taking the chance that your overly enthusiastic hammering will smash into the surrounding wall.

Spackle over the indentations where the screws and nail are, let dry, recoat, and sand smooth when dry.

Excuse Me, but I Think Your Fly Is Open . . . Filling Gaps between Baseboards and Walls

If you have a gap between the wall and the baseboard, you can fill it in by using a caulking gun. The only tricky thing about this lies in making sure that you get a smooth line. The best way to do that is, rather than drawing the gun along the wall toward you, **push** it away from you. In that way, the caulk is forced into the cavity and doesn't bulge so much. Once it's dry, you can paint it.

THE BIG COVER-UP, OR PAINTING

Now that you have successfully prepared your wall surface, you are ready to start painting. What? Oh, Jeni just reminded Joan that a dirty wall makes for dirty paint. (Don't you just hate it when she talks like that? Still, she's right. After all, you wouldn't put on a slinky red silk gown without taking a bath, would you?)

Naturally, there are certain things you need to be mindful of in even this simple process. First of all, *sweep* and *dust* thoroughly. Little dust particles have an absolute mania for freshly painted surfaces and, if they latch onto one, they will leave that oh-so-attractive, pimply surface you all know so well. In addition, if you are about to paint a kitchen or bathroom wall, you need to **scrub** the surfaces with a detergent so that you can remove any trace of grease or mildew that might be lingering. You can use any household detergent, but if you are eco-conscious, don't use a phosphate-based one.

Now, you have to **prepare** your clean surface for the paint it is about to receive. This is especially necessary if you plan on using a high-gloss or enamel-based paint. Paint needs something that will help it to adhere to the wall, and this can be provided by using a **paint de-glosser**. There are several products on the market, but they all contain trisodium phosphate, which is not only superstrong stuff but also carcinogenic, so you must **wear rubber gloves** and make sure you have plenty of ventilation when working with it. A mask would be a good idea, too.

Apply the de-glosser in a thin coat with a rag. Remember, a little goes a long way so, if the surface becomes cloudy, you're using too much. **Trash** the rag when done!

Follow the manufacturer's directions carefully. Some products are no-rinse, some require a drying time before painting, and some should actually still be tacky to the touch when you paint.

Protecting the Innocent . . .
Getting the Room Ready

Jeni's pretty neat when she paints. In other words, paint generally ends up in one of two places, on the wall or on her. Joan, however, has a tendency to let her creative instinct take over to such an extent that little flecks of paint appear everywhere from her toes to Pepper, her dog. Masking tape and drop cloths were invented for people like Joan. Of course, these products are only effective if you use them properly.

Remember, certain things are inevitable in life: death, taxes, and the tendency of paint to splatter. You'll be surprised to see how that little, bitty splatter that fell onto the woodwork from your roller when you were doing the ceiling will eventually turn up as a large, unsightly lump under the finished paint. That unfortunate situation can be avoided by a careful **application of 1-inch masking tape**, pressed into the top edge of the woodwork, forming a ledge, or by **covering the woodwork** with a drop cloth, taped down tightly.

There are some new plastic drop cloths already edged with tape that are designed to be easier to take up afterwards, but Joan found that they stuck more to her feet than the rug. Jeni tries really hard not to laugh when this happens.

Tip #12: Cheap, Cheap, Cheap

When buying plastic drop cloths, check the thickness of the plastic before you plunk down your money. The really inexpensive ones are very thin and a pain to unfold, so if you need to go that route, plan on purchasing an extra one.

Masking is essential if you are working on woodwork or on the part of the wall leading into the woodwork. Make sure that the tape you use doesn't take paint along with it when you rip it off and that your paint surfaces are totally dry before applying it. Putting the tape on properly is time-consuming but will help eliminate the speckled effect in two-tone painting. If you have a steady hand, you can use an *edger* to keep the paint off the wrong surfaces. An edger is simply a thin piece of metal, kind of ruler shaped with a handle. You hold it in one hand, moving it as you paint with the other. There is also a thick plastic strip that you can lay down on the length of your carpet to protect the part of it that comes in contact with the wall from the unwelcome appearance of paint. (Need we tell you which one of us thought to mention this item?)

There is a new product called *Glass Mask* for masking glass that makes painting windows easier. Glass Mask is a thin, waxy film that you roll out then let dry for five to ten minutes. After you're finished painting, it easily scrapes off, along with any paint splatters. There are other liquid masking products that you apply with a brush or sprayer, let dry, and then paint away. When the paint is dry, you should *run a utility knife* around the edge of the trim, then peel the mask off the window. Glass Mask is slightly less work but is more expensive.

If you're painting on the ceiling near a hanging chandelier, a plain old *plastic garbage bag* can be used as a cover. As for the wall lighting switches and outlets, it's a lot easier just to take them off than it is to tape them over. The trick is, every time you unscrew one, put the faceplate and the screws in a plastic bag or wrap them in newspaper. We warn you, if you just set them aside and then move on to the next one, you will forget where you put them. It is just so aggravating to sit back with a proud sigh after you've done all this work, only to discover you have to go to the hardware store and hunt down a screw you KNOW is somewhere in the house. It's also annoying to listen to the chorus of "I told you so's" that usually accompanies this activity.

Also, cover all doors and windows thoroughly; it's easier to pull a bunch of tape off than to scrape paint spatters off.

Tip #13: Do We Hear Spring Cleaning?

The fewer things there are in the room, the easier it will be to move around and paint. Clear the decks of all your precious tchotchkes. (This might be a good time to get rid of all that extra clutter, anyway.) All remaining items of furniture should be moved away from the walls and covered.

Tip #14: Stuck on You

Leaving your masking tape in place is okay for a couple of days, but, in direct sunshine, particularly on windows, a chemical change happens in the glue, making it more difficult to get off. Try to finish the job as quickly as possible, but if you have problems removing the tape, try mineral spirits.

Somewhere over the Rainbow . . . Choosing Your Paint

Okay, now for some of the fun stuff. People usually think of choosing the paint as coming home from the paint store laden down with boxes of those cute little paper swatches that show a color bracketed on either side by slight variations on its theme. While that's the most interesting part, you also have to choose the type of paint you want to use. Generally factored into that decision will be the colors that are then available to you. Ultimately the choice of what color you will use is personal, so we have no tips to help you in that regard. Below we'll concentrate on helping you decide on what type of paint you should buy.

Paint basically comes in two types: **latex or oil based**. Each has advantages and disadvantages, as well as applications they are more suitable for. **Oil-based** paints are harder, stand up to more abuse, and last longer. They also clean well. They are, however, more difficult to paint with, and the cleanup is much more time-consuming. Jeni, who was recycling back in the seventies, has even been known to throw brushes containing oil paint AWAY, rather than face the daunting task of cleaning them.

While **latex or water-based** paints are easy to clean and much easier to apply, their finish is not as tough and they are not as long wearing as the oil-based paints.

For those people who have a sensitivity to some of the substances found in most commercial paints, or for people who simply prefer the choice, there is a third type of paint. This **eco-paint** is of an extremely high quality but, be warned, it is more expensive.

Another determining factor in choosing your type of paint has to do with the finish it will give you. Both oil-based and latex paint come in **flat, semigloss, eggshell**, or **high gloss**. These paints can also contain enamel, which will give a very hard, nonporous surface. Professional painters will tell you that oil is the best way to go. Maybe if you're a pro, but for the rest of the world, latex is just fine. The one room where you might want to seriously consider using oil paint is in the bathroom. Oil paint will stand up to the constant barrage of moisture far better than latex.

Generally speaking, use a **flat paint** on the walls and ceilings and **semigloss or gloss** on the woodwork and trim. If you use a semigloss on the windowsills, use one that has enamel added to it so that it will dry hard enough for things not to stick to it. **Semigloss and high gloss** are almost always used in bathrooms and kitchens because of their higher resistance to stain and the ease with which they can be cleaned up.

As for where to buy your paint, that depends on how much you want to spend. In the world of paint, you pay for what you get. In our experience, the difference between the lowest-cost paints found at a discount store and the middle range or hardware store paint is the amount of coverage you get. And the difference between the midrange paints and the most expensive, paint store variety is the ability of the paint to resist stains and be easily cleaned.

By the way, when you see the words "one coat coverage" written on the can, take that with several grains of salt. Jeni says that she has lived in and painted at least eleven different houses and has never, *ever* been able to get satisfactory results with just one coat. Therefore, before you start, budget into your cost and time that you will probably need at least two coats to get the result you want. If the surface is very dark or if you have virgin (unpainted) wood surfaces that haven't been primed, it'll take three coats. Here's a thought: Since primer is much less expensive than paint, you can save some money by using your primer as your **first coat** and then apply two coats of regular paint on top of it. You will, of course, definitely need to prime ink stains, water marks, or areas covered with rust by using a stain-blocking primer before you paint. If you don't, be prepared to see the little devils bleed right through latex paint. One final thought: When picking a primer, make sure it is for the type of paint—oil or latex, flat or gloss—that you're using. If it isn't clearly marked on the can, ask before you pay.

Tip #15: Profiting from Others' Mistakes

Many hardware and paint stores have what they call "OOPS paint." Sometimes a salesperson will make a mistake when custom mixing a paint or a contractor will return excess paint. These are sold for anywhere between 50 to 80 percent off. It's worth keeping an eye out for something you like, and, if you find something but don't think there's enough at the sale price, the store can always match the rest for you and you'll *still* come out ahead.

How Much Is Too Much, How Little Is Not Enough? . . . Buying the Right Amount

There is nothing worse than slaving like a horse for hours on end to prove to all your friends that you *can* paint your house by yourself, only to discover that you've run out of paint when you still have an area about the size of a large beach ball left over. Unless you have a print in the exact right size and don't mind hanging it on the same level as your sofa, trust us, you will feel like an idiot, so do your calculating before you buy.

A gallon of paint usually covers 300 square feet. To figure out how many gallons you need, measure the length of each wall in feet, add the figures, and multiply this number by the height of your ceiling. This is the *rough square footage* of your walls. Multiply the height and width of any doors, windows, or built-ins that are not being painted, add these figures together, and then subtract the total from the square footage of the walls. This is your *adjusted square footage* for your walls. Multiply the length times the width of the room for the *ceiling square footage*. Add this to your adjusted wall figures and you have the total square footage of the room. Divide this by 300 and you will have the total number of gallons of paint needed for the walls and ceiling.

Unless the paint you are using is very expensive, or you really only need a little to finish, it is rarely worth buying paint by the quart. Instead, buy it in gallons and keep the extra for touch-ups. If you do make a mistake and buy too little, try to finish one wall completely with the paint you have on hand and then start the new paint you have to buy in the corner. That way, if there are any differences in color they will be more easily hidden.

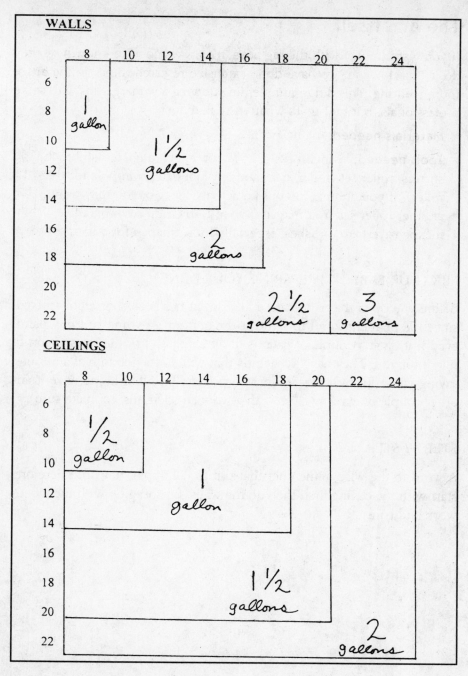

WALLS

CEILINGS

All measurements are in feet.

The Act, Itself

If you want to play with the big boys, it's always good to know how they do it. Just for you, we have done extensive research into the fine art of room painting. This did require tossing down a few margaritas with some professionals, but hey, that's what we're here for.

Materials needed: paint, primer

Tools needed: 3-inch brush, 1 1/2- or 2-inch angled sash brush, stirrers, roller set (roller, pan, and a 4-foot extension pole for the roller). If you are making this an activity for two, you may want another roller set. You may also want to pick up a couple of inexpensive foam brushes, especially those shaped for edging.

MIX IT UP, BABY . . . PREPARING YOUR PAINT

Before you open the paint can, make sure it has been thoroughly mixed, since the pigments tend to settle at the bottom. Anytime you buy paint, even if it's just a couple of gallons of white paint, ask the salesperson to mix it for you. They have a machine that will do the job in half a minute, saving you a lot of labor. When you pry the lid off at home, give it another couple of extra swishes with a wooden stick, just to make sure.

STEP BY STEP

A word to the wise, remember that things fall down, not up. Therefore, start with the ceiling first, then do the walls, finishing up with the woodwork and trim.

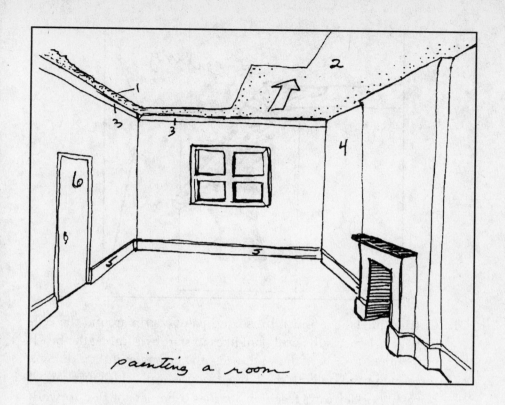

painting a room

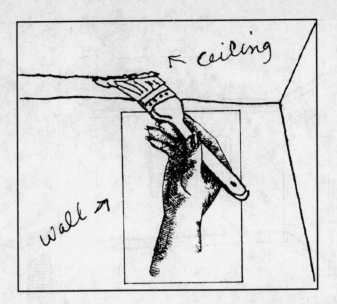

1. **Cutting in.** Take a 3-inch brush and paint a strip around the ceiling where it meets the wall. Jeni likes to start by running the brush in the juncture where the wall meets the ceiling and then doing a three-inch band on both the ceiling and the wall. This takes care of places the roller can't reach and makes a border for you to work within. Like the old bumper car ride at the amusement park, if you try to push the roller too far into the corner, you will hit the other wall and leave skid marks.

2. **Painting the ceiling.** It's usually easier to do this with a 4-foot extension pole than by hoisting yourself up and down a ladder constantly (saves wear and tear on the ol' knees, too). Also, unless your idea of a new coif is to have big blotches of latex paint dotting your part and bangs, it's probably a good idea to cover your head with a hat or scarf. Just pretend it's a fashion statement.

Start in one corner and work your way down the length of the longest wall, painting a three- or four-foot swath as you go. When you reach the opposite wall, turn around and work your way back in another three- or four-foot swath. Continue in this manner until the entire ceiling is done. This technique prevents the roller from leaving lap marks. After the paint is totally dry, apply a second coat.

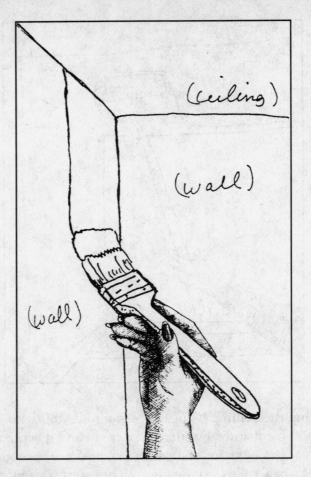

(ceiling)

(wall)

(wall)

3. **Cutting in the walls.** Some suggest doing one wall at a time, but Jeni does them all at once and hasn't had any problems. By the way, Jeni uses the same philosophy for many areas of her life . . . your imagination can fill in the blanks.

   Again, just as you did for the ceiling, take a brush and paint the corners and make a three-inch swath on both walls.

4. **Painting the walls.** The most important part of wall painting is to get even coverage with your roller. The best approach to that end is to first *go up and down*, then *sideways*.

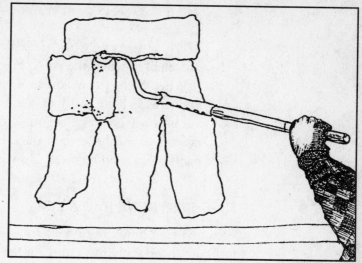

Here's a little bonus tip: Each time, after you first wet the roller, run it up the wall, not down so that the paint will be less likely to drip down the wall. If you consistently have a problem with gobs of paint flying everywhere, you're using too much. Get rid of some of the excess by pressing very lightly and then try to be more judicious on the next go-around.

Tip #16: Pouring It On

When filling a roller pan, only pour in enough paint to cover the bottom third of the pan. That way, there is plenty of room to spread the paint evenly on the roller and to get rid of any excess.

5. **Painting the woodwork.** The woodwork refers to anything made of wood (like, duh!) and includes the baseboards as well as windowsills. Do not even think of starting this until after the wall paint is totally dry. If you start too soon, one color will run into the other and you'll have a total mess on your hands. This is especially true when you are using a different color for the woodwork than for the

walls. Yes, this IS another thing we know from experience, so stop snickering!

While the woodwork is usually done with a brush, you can also use small rollers if the wood boards are wide enough.

When doing the windows, if yours are double hung, raise the bottom sash as high as it will go and then lower the outer, top sash as low as it will go. Paint the top sash first, then the inside sash that you raised previously. Reverse them back to their normal positions and paint the remaining areas. Now paint the sills and window frames.

MISTAKES, WE'VE HAD A FEW

We don't care how careful you are; sometimes things happen. Like, you just got too fed up with waiting for the first coat to dry so you went ahead and did the second one, anyway. That terribly unattractive-looking finish that resembles dry, cracked skin is called **alligatoring**. If it's not too bad, you can get away with just sanding it down and then filling in the puckered parts with a spackling compound, waiting for it to dry, and then re-painting. If it looks like hell, you're out of luck. You have to strip the whole thing off and start again. . . . See, patience *can* be a virtue.

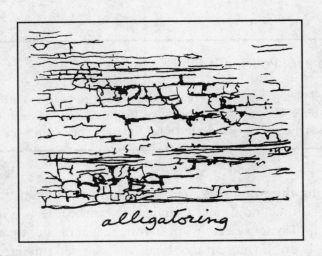

alligatoring

If you painted in a room that gets direct sunlight, you might notice a **blistering** effect in your paint surface. This happened when the external layer of paint dried faster than what was underneath. Before you do anything, wait for the whole thing to dry hard to the touch, then scrape away the blisters, sand, and repaint. A word to the wise, here: Try to keep the blinds or curtains drawn for the next time so that the room stays cooler.

blistering

If you have blobs of paint in your surface or if there are **driplike ridges** in several places, you applied the paint too thickly in that area. Sand the blobs off when they are dry and repaint *lightly* over the places where they appeared. In the future, you can avoid this kind of problem by making sure that you start with just a light coating on the brush and that all excess paint is dabbled off. On the other hand, if the whole surface has the **wrinkled** texture of an old prune, you used too thick a coat all over the place and you will now have to sand the whole thing down and try again, using much less paint, if you please.

After all this you may be wondering, Why would anyone go to all the trouble of painting themselves when they could just hire someone else to do the job? Well, for one thing, painters can be expensive and, for another, while the work is somewhat tedious, it really isn't all that difficult and is one of the fastest, most cost-efficient ways to change your home exactly the way you want it done.

CLEANING UP

In a later chapter on cleanup techniques, we'll describe the best way to clean up brushes and other paint-related paraphernalia. One thing to keep in mind, however, is that it is a hell of a lot easier to do it as you go along than wait until you're all finished. Take a second to wash off that brush as soon as you're done with it. Paint hardens fast, so if your idea of cleaning up is throwing out, we hope you have a relative in the paint business who can keep you supplied.

If you need to take a break during the job, wrap the roller and brushes in plastic wrap or foil and set them out of the sun. If you're using latex and plan on stopping until the next day, the roller and brushes will need to be cleaned. The roller can be cleaned more easily if you take the cover off and wash it separately. There is a device called a *spinner* that will get rid of most of the water in the roller, but we usually just leave it to drain standing upright, then finish drying it with paper towels. It isn't a perfect method, but it works and we don't have to buy something else to fiddle with and to store somewhere.

Brushes that have been used with oil-based paint can be put in a jar of *mineral spirits* and left for a day or two. You'll need to find a way to support the brush so it doesn't rest on the bottom, thereby bending the bristles. Jeni found that the easiest thing to do is to cut a hole in the lid and push the brush handle through that and then screw the lid back on the jar. Make sure that the bristles are fully immersed in the mineral spirits. The same thing can be done with rollers in a five-gallon bucket. When you are ready to resume painting, shake most of the spirits out, then use paper towels to remove the rest. Please remember to dispose of towels, rags, mineral spirits, and paint properly, as hazardous waste.

Tip #17: Book That Manicure, Now!

To prevent paint from getting under your nails and in your cuticles, rub petroleum jelly around and under your nails, then gently wipe off any that's on your hands. When you are finished painting, wipe the rest of the Vaseline off and the paint will come with it.

Fancy Shmancy . . . Decorative Techniques

Now that you've gotten the bug, you might want to explore the idea of doing something extra special to the areas you are painting. While there are many excellent books that go into the area of decorative painting in some detail, here are a few ideas we would like to share with you.

We've already mentioned above that you can accent a room simply by painting the baseboards and door trims a different color from the walls. This is one of the simplest things to do and can solve the problem of being afraid to do a small room in a color other than white. Joan left her small den painted white but did the woodwork and door trim in a medium gray/blue, which picked up a color that ran through her floor tile. Rather than make the room look smaller, it added definition.

Other easy-to-do ideas include:

Marbleizing Staircases: There is a special can of spray paint on the market that you use for this project. The paint inside is a mixture of a base color like white or black and another contrasting paint that comes out in long strings of gray on white or white on black. You can use the paint on metal, wood, ceramic, or any painted surface. You point it where you want it to go and move the can around so that the string of paint comes out in a circular manner. It's a little bit like playing with "Silly String" and produces a marblelike effect.

Stencils: Most art supply houses carry stencils in a variety of shapes and designs. These are especially fun to use if you are decorating a child's room. Once your paint surface has dried thoroughly, you can put the stencil of the truck, horse, or star in place and paint inside it in any color you want. It really helps to give an individual look to a bedroom or kitchen.

Tromp l'Oeil: Put simply, this means a trick to the eye and is a technique made famous in places like the Palace of Versailles. *Trompe l'Oeil* creates an illusion of space and texture. While decorators often use expensive artists who can create the illusion of an open window or an ocean view, for your purposes, taking a sponge or rag and dappling paint onto your newly painted and dried wall surface can give the illusion of texture that can resemble anything from fabric to marble to stucco. Start off light and easy and you can always add as you go along. Remember, less is more.

Spray Paints: This is an easy way to spruce up a piece of wood furniture or an old wicker chair, but make sure that you cover the area under the object you are spraying or else, well, we're sure that by now you've got the picture, right?

TAKE FIVE

There really is nothing like a new coat of paint to make you feel as if you live in a new place. We're not being delusional, or anything—we swear it's true. By the way, keep a can of the paint you used handy so you can do touch-ups, too. Those of you with children, we're sure, have some idea of what an attraction freshly painted walls have for tiny, smudgy hands. Oh, well, it was nice while it lasted, wasn't it?

6

Come On, Baby, Light My World

ELECTRICAL REPAIRS AND REWIRING

Let's shed a little light on the subject. (Sorry, couldn't resist.) This chapter is tricky. It is designed to help you with *basic* repairs and improvements. Our aim, here, is not to have you tackle any of the major remodeling or rewiring at your humble abode because electricity can kill you and, let's face it, we don't want that much bad Karma on our heads. So, for the really big and critical stuff, we would caution all but the most experienced do-it-yourselfers: Get help.

If you are feeling adventurous, however, please note that, although most communities have adopted the National Electrical Code, regulations do differ across the country. Not everything sold in a hardware store will necessarily meet local requirements, so check with an expert. In addition, if you are altering existing wiring or adding new wires, you will need to obtain permits and get inspected. Don't be tempted to bypass this step if it is required by the building department since, safety issues aside, it could affect your future ability to improve or sell your home. Specifically, when you want to do further remodeling, if it is discovered that permits were not obtained the first time, you could be forced to demolish all your hard work, file plans and permits, and start over. Worse still, if, when you go to sell it, the improvements you made are deemed illegal, your buyer could ask to be reimbursed for your error.

That having been said, there are still lots of projects you can do on your own safely and easily. These are:

1. Repair plugs and lamp sockets.
2. Repair wall switches and convert them to three-way grounded switches.
3. Add track lighting or dimmers.
4. Replace outlets and ceiling fixtures with new ones.

You can also add switches and outlets to what you already have, but, before you do so, make sure that your circuits can handle the increased power demands. Once again, check your local building codes to determine whether permits are needed and if you must use a licensed electrician.

Tip #1: Dumb-Blonde Jokes Aren't Funny

If something isn't working, check the obvious before you call for help. Funnily enough, electricians report that often they respond to a frantic call from someone claiming that their appliance isn't working only to discover that it wasn't plugged in. Sooooo . . . unless you want to be the subject of a good yuk at the next meeting of the local union, check before you call.

BABY STEPS

The first step in any electrical repair is to **shut off the current**. You are not Benjamin Franklin out testing a kite; electricity *does* flow through the wires, so don't be stupid. You can turn off the power by going to the fuse box or main service panel and either pulling the fuse or switching off the circuit breaker. Although you only need to shut off the specific circuit or fuse that controls the power source where you will be working, if you can't identify which one goes where, you can turn off the main power instead. By the way, just so you don't have to go through the same ordeal the next time this happens, it's probably a good idea to make a diagram of your circuits so you know what's connected to what. This could be another one of those fun activities you can do with your significant other since it's easier to do with two people instead of one. All that it involves is turning off one switch at a time and checking to see what part of the house has lost power. Having someone helping inside saves a lot of running back and forth.

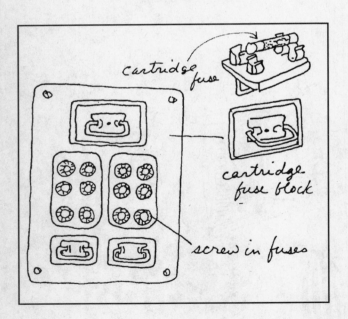

cartridge fuse

cartridge fuse block

screw in fuses

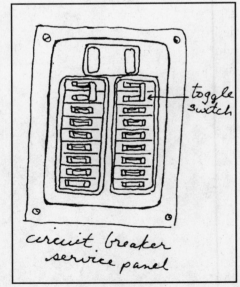

toggle switch

circuit breaker service panel

Safety Tips

As you learned in school, electricity travels along the path of least resistance back to the earth. This is why newer wiring always has three wires: *a hot wire*—usually black, which carries current from the source; *a neutral wire*—usually white, which returns the current; and a green or bare copper wire, which is the *"ground" wire.* Should there be a short circuit, the electrical current will flow along the ground wires safely, preventing shock or fire. It's very important to follow all directions and reconnect the ground wires when doing any electrical work. If you are not sure about something, call an electrician!

If your fuse blows or circuit breaker trips, try turning off the appliance(s) or moving them to another line. Then reset the circuit or fuse. If it blows again, you could have a short; in which case, call an electrician right away.

Basic Techniques

There are a few things you will need to do for almost any kind of electrical repair you intend to make: *Testing for power* is essential since it is detrimental to your overall life expectancy on this earth to do any repairs with the power still on. Therefore, you'd better be 100 percent certain that it is really off when you want it to be. You will also need to know about *stripping, splitting*, and *connecting wires,* as these techniques are, likewise, part of your electricity ABC's.

TESTING FOR POWER

There are two kinds of devices commonly used when making electrical repairs. The first is a *neon tester*. It has two probes and a lightbulb and is used to see if current is present in the outlets, switches, and lights. You test for electricity by inserting the two probes in the socket. If the bulb lights, you have power and you *must* shut it off before you touch the wires.

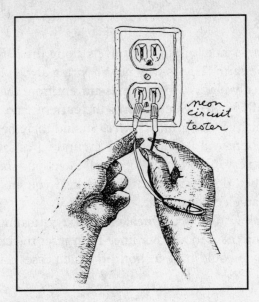

neon
circuit
tester

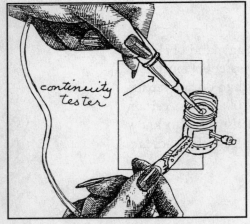

continuity
tester

A **continuity tester** is only used when the **power is turned off**. Its purpose is to figure out if a switch or socket is broken inside. Therefore, in addition to two probes and a lightbulb, it has its own small power source. If you place a probe at each end of a lamp socket and the tester lights up, the socket is working and you are in business.

STRIPPING, SPLITTING, AND CONNECTING WIRES

Don't Tug So Hard . . . Replacing Plugs on Cords

Jeni has a confession to make: "I am a cord yanker. I don't do it often and never when someone else is around, but sometimes I just take that sucker and pull it out of the wall by the cord." Well, Joan, for one, is shocked. Is there a twelve-step program for that? If you, too, are a cord yanker, that might account for some of the pretty scary-looking ancient lamps you've got hanging around. If they look anything like the ones we've seen, you wouldn't want to be holding on to their plugs when the power gets turned on. Whether it's a worn-out, cracked, or melted plug; frayed wires; or just an old Mateus bottle you want to turn into a lamp, putting a plug on the end of a wire is a pretty good place to start getting you comfortable with electrical repairs.

Materials needed: new plug

Tools needed: screwdriver, needle-nose pliers, combination tool

When it comes to new plugs, don't get creative. You should replace a flat plug with a flat plug, a three prong with another three prong, and so on.

Quick Connect

The easiest and newest plug on the market is called a "quick connect" plug.

Cut the old plug off the cord, but don't strip the wires. Holding the prongs, pull them out of the casing. Push the wire through the hole in the back of the casing. Push the prongs apart, then feed the cord into the back of the plug. When you push the prongs back together, small spikes on the inside edge of the prongs will dig into the wires inside. Slide the plug back into the casing. Presto! You're ready to go.

Flat Cord

If you use a regular flat cord, cut the old plug off, then pull the two wires apart with your fingers. If this is hard, lay the wire flat, and using a **Mack knife**, cut through the groove in the middle. About three or four inches should give you enough room to hold the wire while stripping the insulation. The easiest way to strip the insulation is by using a combination tool, but you can also use the Mack knife to shave the insulation off. You should have about three-quarters of an inch of bare wire. Twist the strands together.

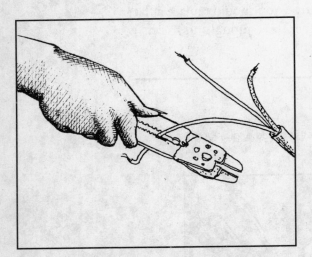 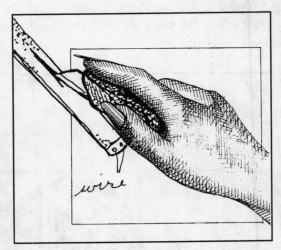

Remove the screw from the top of the plug and separate the pieces. Wrap the copper wire around the screw terminals inside the plug clockwise. Tighten the screws. Put the top back on and reassemble.

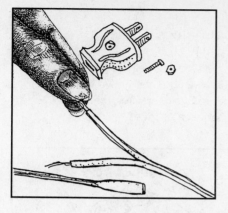

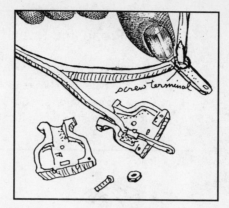

screw terminal

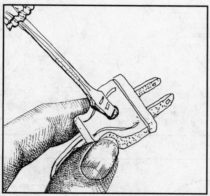

Three-Prong and Round-Cord Plugs

The cords on these plugs are generally round, heavier than the others, and have two layers of insulation. Strip about two inches of the outer insulation so you can get to the inner wires, then strip about three-quarters of an inch off of each of these.

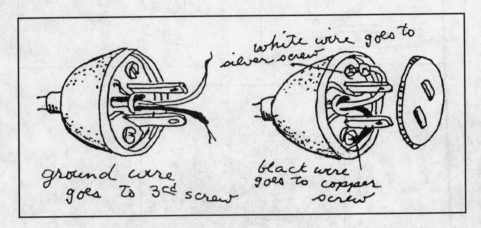

white wire goes to silver screw

ground wire goes to 3ᵈ screw

black wire goes to copper screw

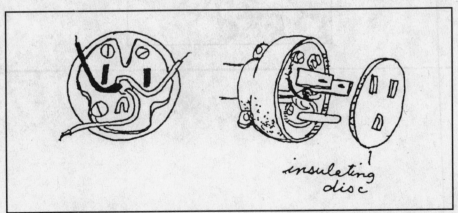

insuleting disc

Take the *faceplate* off the back of the new plug, then insert the wires. It's a good idea to tie the black and white wires with an underwriter's knot so they can't get pulled out of the plug.

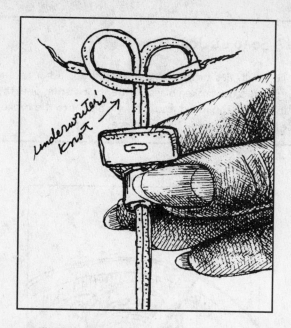

Using **needle-nose pliers**, hook the black wire clockwise around the brass screw and the white wire around the silver screw. *The ground wire should be attached to the ground screw.* Tighten the screws, but make sure no bare wires touch each other. If you find you've stripped too much, just loosen the screws and trim the ends.

Put the faceplate back on.

ONE IF BY LAND . . . LAMP REPAIR

Lamp Sockets

Most sockets are interchangeable, so if you have one with a pull chain and you want to switch to a twist knob or vice versa, it shouldn't be a problem. Just remember always to unplug the lamp before you remove the shade and bulb.

Tip #2: Soap du Jour

If the lightbulb has broken in the socket, use a bar of soap by pressing it onto the broken glass and gently twisting until the bulb lifts out. Or you can insert another lightbulb into the broken one and use it to unscrew the broken piece.

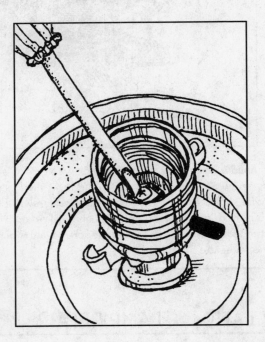

In the center of the socket you'll see a metal contact tab. First, gently scrape it with a screwdriver, then pry it up slightly. Put the bulb back in and check to see if the lamp now works. If not, unplug and carry on.

The socket has an outer metal case. This is either marked *"press"* or, if it is an older lamp, will simply have screws at the bottom. Squeeze at the markings or unscrewing and carefully, lift the case off. If the cardboard underneath is damaged, you must replace the socket as the cardboard is needed for insulation. (By the way, when you buy a new socket, make sure it's got the same amp and volt ratings as the previous one.)

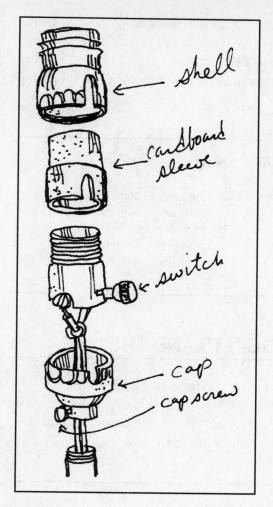

shell

cardboard sleeve

switch

cap

cap screw

If the cardboard is not damaged, remove it and check to see if the wires are securely fastened to the screws. If they are loose, tighten, reassemble, and try the lamp again. If the wires are not loose, proceed straight to the next step.

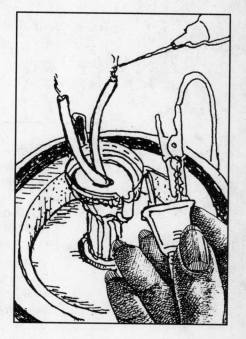

Using a *continuity tester*, check the wires. Do this by clipping the tester to one prong of the plug, then touch each of the exposed wires at the other end of the cord. Switch the clip to the other prong, then test the wires again. If the tester doesn't light up either way, the cord and or plug is bad and needs replacing. If the cord is good, your problem is with the socket and you will have to replace it.

When you look at the lamp wire, you'll see that one side of the insulation is ridged, the other smooth. The smooth wire should be attached to the brass screw, the ridged wire to the silver.

Put it all back together, making sure you put the cardboard insulating sleeve back on.

Tip #3: Such a Bargain . . . Not!

A word to the wise: Those of you who are lucky enough to travel to Europe, try to resist buying any of those adorable antique lamps you see in flea markets. The electrical current is totally different and not something you can adapt yourself. You might end up spending a bundle getting it fixed, and then your nifty little "find" won't seem like such a bargain after all.

CHANGING WALL SOCKETS AND THE LIKE

You guys are doing great, so let's move on to some bigger stuff.

Replacing a wall receptacle (socket) or switch is really no more complicated than repairing a lamp; it just feels that way because it's part of a bigger system, the whole house. So, into the breach we go.

Tip #4: Better Safe Than Sorry

In addition to replacing faulty receptacles, you may want to replace your receptacles in order to accommodate three-prong plugs or, for safety reasons, to install a ground fault circuit interrupter (GFI) in the bathroom or kitchen. A GFI is very sensitive to power surges and is designed to shut off before a shock occurs. Because water and electrical appliances are often found together, GFI's are now routinely installed in kitchens and bathrooms. Whenever you replace an outlet, you should make sure the ratings for the amps, volts, and wiring are the same.

Tip #5: Hitting the Ground

If you replace an old-style two-pronged outlet, make sure the outlet is grounded first. To do this, use a **neon circuit tester**. Place one
probe in the plug and touch the other to the coverplate screw. The
outlet is grounded if the bulb lights up. Otherwise, do not replace
the outlet; call an electrician to retrofit!

Receptacles

Materials needed: new receptacle

Tools needed: screwdriver, masking tape, circuit tester

As usual, unless you want to be toast, shut the power off.

Remove the screw in the middle of the coverplate, then pry the plate off.
Use a circuit tester to check for current. To do this, touch top screws on both
sides with the probe, then repeat with the bottom screw. If it doesn't light,
all's well and it's safe to work. If it does, check the power source, again.

Undo the mounting screws and pull the receptacle out from the wall. At
this point you will be able to see exactly how the wires are connected. *This
is a very important thing to note!* For example, the wiring will be different
if your receptacle is the **last** on an electrical line than if it is in the **middle**.

The diagrams below show how the connections work.

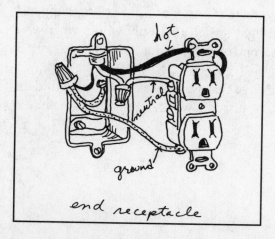

end receptacle

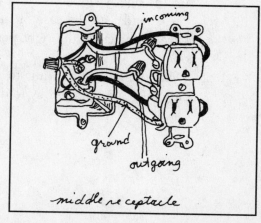

middle receptacle

Tip #6: Connecting the Dots

It's a good idea to label each wire before you undo it. That way, you'll know exactly how to hook it back up. This is intricate stuff, and you certainly don't want to have to do it twice.

Unhook the wires by either loosening the screws, or if it is a "push in" connection, undo it by pushing the tip of a small screwdriver into the slot.

Attach the wires to the new receptacle, then connect the ground wire (remember it's either a green insulated wire or a bare copper wire) to the ground screw terminal.

Slide the receptacle back into the wall, gently pushing the wires into the back of the box. Screw in the mounting screws, then the coverplate screw.

Wall Switches

Picture this scene: You are coming home to your dark apartment on a cold and rainy winter night. Your hands are laden down with bags of groceries, your briefcase, and the soggy umbrella you bought when you came out of the subway that has since turned inside out twice in the block and a half you walked to get home. As your hand gropes blindly for the light switch, you find it, switch it on, and . . . nothing happens! Yes, friends, it's the case of the light switch that only works when you have it in exactly the right position (or if the moon is in Taurus, either one).

We think it's about time to change that wayward switch so, to find an easy and inexpensive way to do it, just follow the yellow brick road.

Tip #7: Switching Made Easy

There are several different kinds of switches: ***single pole, three way***, and ***four way***. Each, respectively, has two, three, or four screw terminals. The three- and four-way switches are used to control an outlet or light from more than one location, such as a hall light you can turn on from the top of the stairs or the bottom. A new switch *must* be the same type as the old.

If you have a three-way or four-way pole, you will have to check *each* with a continuity tester in order to find the faulty switch.

STEP BY STEP

Materials needed: replacement switch

Tools needed: screwdriver, circuit tester, continuity tester

Begin by removing the faceplate (after you've turned the power off, of course!). Undo the mounting screws and pull the switch out from the wall. Be careful not to touch any bare wires or the terminals. Using a current tester, take one probe and touch it to the screw terminal that the black wire is attached to. Then place the other probe on the metal box or bare ground wire. Repeat with the other side. If it doesn't light up, there's no current and it's safe to proceed. If not, you haven't turned the power off. Do so, please!

Sometimes the problem at the switch is just a loose wire; try checking that out, first. If the wiring is secure, proceed. If it's loose, tighten and put the switch back together and see if it works. If not, you'll need a new **switch mechanism**.

Label the wires and disconnect them from the old switch and then attach wires to the new switch. If

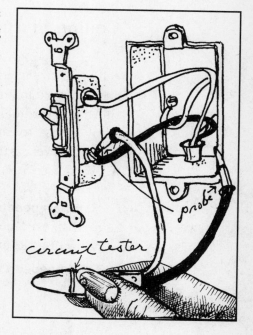

there is a green ground screw on the new switch, attach the ground wire in the box to it.

Slide the switch back into the wall, gently pushing the wires into the back. Secure the mounting screw and put the coverplate back on.

DIMMER SWITCHES

Nothing creates a romantic mood better than a dimmer switch. These are installed pretty much the same way as a regular switch. In fact, you must replace a two-way, three-way, or four-way switch with the same type of dimmer. So, if you have a three-way switch, use a three-way dimmer. It will have an extra wire: if it's red, connect it to the black circuit wire. If the dimmer wire is a green ground wire, it should be connected to the metal box or circuit ground wire.

HENNY PENNY, CALL YOUR OFFICE . . . REPLACING CEILING FIXTURES AND FANS

Ceiling Fixtures

Is there a special store where apartment builders go to buy the ugliest ceiling fixture imaginable? Every time Joan has moved into a new place she is amazed to find, plunk dab in the middle of her dining room, something left over from a Gaudy R Us garage sale. Change it. After all, you're going to have to eat under that thing, so make it something that is pleasing to the eye, fits the rest of your decor, and doesn't look like a relic from a 1970s disco.

Materials needed: wire nuts and new fixture. P.S.: You might need an extra body to help you hold it up, too, if the fixture is heavy or awkward.

Tools needed: ladder, screwdriver, circuit tester, continuity tester

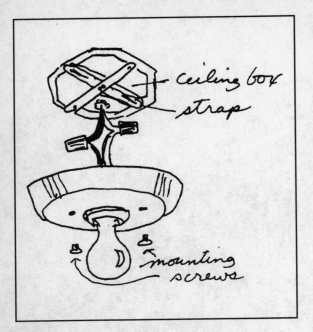

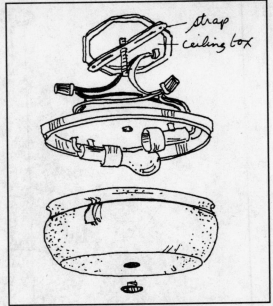

Turn off the power. Remove shade by undoing the screws either at the sides or bottom, depending on the type. The metal fixture underneath is set against the ceiling by mounting screws. Usually you can twist them off, but you may have to unscrew them.

At this point, you may discover that the fixture is stuck to the ceiling by layers of paint. Before you try to pry it off, take a utility knife and run it around the base of the fixture, cutting through any paint or tape there. If you are not careful about how you do this, the paint may crack or, if you have Sheetrock ceilings, the surface may tear. In any case, it will be a mess and you will have a far bigger job on your hands to repair.

There will usually be only two wires inside, connected to two wires in the ceiling by electrical tape or wire nuts. Undo these connections and remove the fixture.

All new fixtures come with directions. Basically you're working backwards from what you just did, reattaching the wires, rehanging the base to the ceiling, screwing the lightbulb in, and replacing the shade.

Ceiling Fans

Casablanca, anyone? For a bit of a tropical feel as well as a way to help circulate the air, nothing can beat an overhead fan. They are hung exactly the same way as lighting fixtures, but, before you buy one, make sure the ceiling can support the weight and that the wiring is rated for the power the fan will require. If you don't, you will have one nasty hole over your head and probably a lawsuit from the person who was sitting under it when it fell. Because of the weight involved, this is another job that will require a buddy.

READY FOR MY CLOSE-UP, MR. DEMILLE . . . LIGHTING DESIGN

Lighting can instantly create a mood, show off a treasured possession, or even make as simple a task as working in the kitchen easier. Throwing a shawl over a lamp may have worked for Blanche DuBois, but it isn't always appropriate.

In any room, there are three kinds of lighting:

General—for overall illumination, as in a ceiling fixture
Task—light specifically for a purpose such as reading, putting on makeup, etc.
Accent—designed to illuminate a particular object or area, such as a piece of art or a group of plants

Once you figure out your lighting needs, you will have an easier time determining what type of lighting you should add or change.

General Lighting

Do you remember the interrogation scene in old police movies when a lightbulb was aimed into the face of the accused murderer to get him to confess? Well, general and overhead lighting isn't quite that bad, but it's a close second. You can improve the effect, however, if you place the lights in a triangle pattern so that the illuminated area is actually lit from three sources. The result will be much easier on the eyes and will eliminate the glare created by single or overhead lighting.

For the purposes of this chapter, we will only deal with ways to change your general lighting externally; i.e., not within the wiring system of the house. *Track lighting* is an excellent solution to the problem, as it provides overhead lighting that you can set up to suit your specific needs. In our project section we will go into detail on how to install track lighting, which is one of the most popular styles of lighting design around. It works especially well with high ceilings and modern decor.

Putting in recessed lighting is a much bigger deal that usually requires the help of a professional. Joan has an interesting system in her high-ceilinged living room which was created by drilling holes into opposing walls, inserting poles, and stringing special wire to connect them. The wire carries the current from which high-tech-looking halogen bulbs are hung like laundry on a line. When the wall switch is turned on, the current is activated in the wire and the lights all turn on. It's really dramatic and almost looks like a sculpture. It was pretty easy to do but, although she would like to take credit for it, she can't. It was one of the legacies of her marriage. Say what you will, she says about her ex, he was very handy with current. (Jeni just added a very snide "And currency," but that's another book.)

Task Lighting

The bathroom and the kitchen are two places where people usually get the most out of improving the lighting.

Since in older homes the bathrooms often have only one ceiling light, you can start your retrofitting there. When you do any work in the bathroom, it's best to install GFI's on all the outlets. Bathrooms usually need at least an overhead ceiling light and lighting around the mirror. When designing the lights around the mirror, think about placing them at average eye level, about sixty inches high and thirty inches apart to avoid glare. Another easy option is to put a strip of light over the sink. These strips come already assembled with anywhere from four to six bulbs per fixture. If you already have some kind of light over the sink, it is easy to convert it to the strip. If no light exists, you will probably have to hire an electrician to install new wiring. Occasionally, you may need a light in the tub or shower area. Any light installed over the tub or shower should be encased in something waterproof.

The easiest way to upgrade the lighting in your kitchen is to add fluorescent lights under your wall cabinets. They go up quickly and can be plugged into a wall socket or wired into a switch. Locate them closer to the front than the back of the cabinets. If the tube is visible, you can always hide it behind a small valence. You'll be amazed at the difference this light makes. Each kit comes with the fixture, the lightbulb, and a couple of screws to attach them to the undersides of your cabinets. They're very lightweight and easy to attach.

Other areas where task lighting is helpful include the spaces over the sink, stove, and kitchen table.

The chandelier over your dining room table is yet another example of task lighting. If you are going to install a new one, there are a few technical ideas to keep in mind before you make your new purchase: The scale of the chandelier should be in balance with the room and the table beneath it. A good rule of thumb is that the length of the chandelier in inches should be no more than the diagonal of the room is in feet. Its width should not be more than the width of the table minus twelve inches. Also check that, at its lowest point, it is thirty to thirty-six inches from the table. That will help to avoid head bumping on the part of your dinner guests.

Sometimes it's hard to find a chandelier that illuminates both the table and the room since they are often either too bright or not bright enough. You can solve this problem by installing a dimmer switch to regulate the degree of light yourself. Another possibility is to add wall sconces or side lamps and put low-wattage bulbs in the chandelier.

Accent Lights

If you are setting up an accent light, you can use a single lamp or one or two overheads (like two track light cells) angled toward each other and aimed to surround an object or painting in a bath of light. Halogen lighting is especially good for this since you can control the angle of light more easily than with a more traditional bulb. Also, since the light in a halogen lamp is designed to bounce off the ceiling and radiate down, you will have, in effect, created a curtain of light around your object.

TAKE FIVE

Well, if you're reading this we assume you survived your introduction to the world of electricity in a manner that would make old Ben Franklin proud. In other words, you turned off the power before you did anything and made sure you understood which wires were which, and didn't kill anyone in the process. (When he says he wants you to "turn him on," just know that he doesn't mean that in the literal sense.)

Basically, that's the most important thing to remember about the topic for the simpler stuff. For real problems with circuits and fuses and such, don't screw around; call the pros.

For now, practice the tasks outlined above and join us in the project chapter for instructions on how to lay in track lighting.

CHAPTER

7

Drilling Is My Passion

HOW TO PUT UP SHELVES AND OTHER DRILL USES

Now, we don't know about you, but we heard that men find the prospect of seeing a woman with a power tool in her hands incredibly sexy. It probably has something to do with their mothers, but, beyond that, we're not sure we should go there.

While that's not the only reason to get comfortable with a drill, since its use as a sexual aid is probably more theoretical than practical, we do want to welcome you with open arms to the wonderful world of power. Once you have overcome whatever fear you might have about using a drill, you won't be able to get through any project without one.

Modern drills are not only good for their time-honored skill in making holes but, with their various attachments, they can take on the identity of just about any other tool from screwdriver to sander to polisher.

In this chapter, however, we want to show you the most typical ways you will use a drill—for making holes and putting up shelves.

PLAYING IT SAFE

1. You know how you should never pull a cat by its tail? Well, never hold a drill by its cord. If you happen to be doing so and it accidentally turns on, then prepare for one wild ride!

2. Since you will probably need to use an extension cord to get from the outlet to the thing that needs drilling, make sure that you are using a heavy-duty extension cord, not a household one that might not be able to stand up to the power. Oh yeah: Never wear long necklaces or loose scarves while working with a drill. The Isadora Duncan look might be fun at parties, but here it could be deadly.

3. Unplug all power tools before changing the blades, bits, and accessories.

4. Use goggles where advised.

5. Always use the chuck to tighten the drill; fingers are a definite no-no.

A LITTLE BIT OFF THE TOP . . .
WHAT YOU'LL NEED

As we mentioned in the chapter on tools, drills come in many prices and with a varied assortment of bells and whistles. For your purposes, a moderately priced, 3/8-inch variable-speed, reversible drill will pretty much do anything you are likely to encounter, plus they're easy to handle and extremely useful. In general, drill motors range from 1/3 horse power (hp) to 3/8 plus, but 1/3 to 1/2 hp should be sufficient. If you have the option, a cordless drill is a great addition to any tool chest, as it gives you added flexibility as to where you can drill and is much lighter than the standard variety.

A drill does not work without bits. The standard set we described in the tools section is your best bet as a start-up, plus if the walls in your home are made of either stone, brick, or concrete, you'll need a set of **masonry bits** as well. For plasterboard or wood walls, a set of **wood bits**, 1/16- to 1/4-inch should suffice.

We find that **magnetized screwdriver heads** really help if you need to screw in tight areas (get your mind out of the gutter, Jeni). One flat and one Phillips screwdriver drill head should do the trick. If you want to countersink screws in wood, you can buy a bit for that specific purpose, too.

DOING THAT THING YOU DO . . .
THE "HOW TO" OF IT

Frankly, drilling a hole is not exactly brain surgery, but there are a few basics to keep in mind. Simpleminded as this might seem, it's important to drill a straight hole. If your drilling technique resembles that of a snake charmer and your drill starts to wiggle toward its target as soon as it touches the wall, it will be very hard to get the screw in straight and things will go downhill from there.

That having been said, however, we should let you in on a deep, dark secret about a friend of ours whom, for the purposes of this story, we will call . . . uhm . . . "not-Joan" (she's starting to feel picked on).

One day, while "not-Joan" was standing around her kitchen with nothing to do, she noticed that there were no pulls on any of her cabinet drawers. Now, it's not as if she had any trouble opening them or anything (all she had to do was put her fingers under the groove specially made for that purpose and pull), but she thought that having nice knobs on her drawers would improve the look of her kitchen.

She went to several kitchen stores and came home with samples of different drawer pulls to see which one would look best. After making her selection, she bought enough for twelve drawers, returned the rest, and came home in gleeful expectation of the task ahead. But, after she had marked off places where the pulls were to go and had revved up her drill, she ran into a big problem . . . her bit wouldn't go through the wood. Not realizing she didn't have the correct bits, she pushed and shoved and was finally able to get some of them through, but the sizes of the holes were all askew from her effort and she broke three bits in the process. Discouraged, she stopped dead in her tracks and abandoned her project. To this date, her kitchen looks like a drawer pull graveyard—some drawers have pulls on straight, some have their pulls leaning at an angle, and some have no pulls at all.

How sad. How very, very sad.

So, the moral here is **Plan ahead**. Measure carefully and make sure that the size of the drill bit you use is right for the hole you want to make. If you are going to be putting in a screw, the hole, the bit, *and* the screw have to match.

By the way, once you have done all your preparatory work, then and only then can you even think about turning on the power. **Start out slowly,** increasing the speed as the bit catches. If the drill bit tends to slide upon entry, you can either put a small piece of **masking tape over the hole** and drill through it or buy an **"auger" bit**. These special bits have a very sharp point that grabs the wood fast. You can also tap the point of the screw into the wood with a hammer to mark your place and then drill. When predrilling for screws, always choose a bit that is smaller than the shank of the screw, or else the screw will disappear into the wall, never to be found again.

GETTING ATTACHED . . . SECURING THINGS TO WALLS AND CEILINGS

Lightweight things can be attached to the wall directly, but heavier objects should be attached to the **studs** in the wall for added strength. When your walls were built, the studs were placed at regular intervals, usually about sixteen or twenty-four inches apart. You can find them by tapping on the wall and listening for changes in sound, or by a **stud finder**, available in any hardware store. . . . All right, ladies, let's not start a stampede here. They only work for one kind of stud!

By and large, with the exception of pictures, *don't use nails to hang things on walls*. **Screws, anchors, and bolts** are much more secure and will not pull away from the wall. Plastic anchors and screws work well for medium loads like curtains, but something like a hanging plant needs a heavy-duty toggle bolt. Anchors come prepackaged and give a description of the loads they can safely hold.

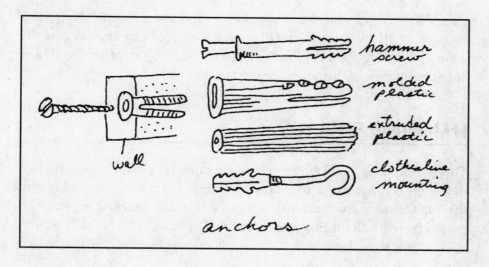

wall

hammer screw

molded plastic

extruded plastic

clothesline mounting

anchors

To use a plastic anchor and screw, **mark the position of the holes**. Select a drill bit that is as close to the size of the anchor as possible. Occasionally, this will be indicated on the package, but if you have to guess, it is better to go too small than too large. If you do make a mistake, how-

ever, and end up with a hole the size of the Grand Canyon, don't worry—
just patch it up, let it dry, and redrill.

Insert the anchor directly into the hole so that the plastic circle is flush
with the wall, then screw directly into it.

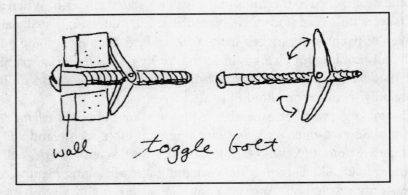

When using a *toggle bolt*, choose a drill bit the same size as the *widest
point* of the folded-down wings of the bolt. You'll need a bit that is larger
than a quarter of an inch, and should probably use a *"spade"* bit for this
purpose. *Drill* away, then *insert* the collapsed bolt into the hole and the
wings will spring open behind the surface of the wall or ceiling, grabbing
onto the interior of the hole and locking it in place.

HANGING SHELVES

There are two kinds of bookshelves: *Freestanding,* which, as the name
indicates, is made up of supports and shelves that form a portable unit
that stands away from a wall, and those that are *attached* to and supported by the wall. In this chapter, we will speak about the latter kind.

Here you have the choice of three different types of systems.

1. *Wooden strips*—usually require three walls for strength.
2. *Adjustable strips*—go against a back wall and have brackets that
   hold up the shelves.
3. *L-shaped or triangular brackets*—attach both to the back wall and
   bottom side of the shelf. These come in a variety of styles and ma-

terials that run the gamut from basic gray metal to decorative wood and iron brackets.

Wooden Strips

Shelves hung with wooden strips must be supported at the side and, unless the shelf is short, also at the back.

1. Measure the width of the shelf and the length.
2. Cut two strips of one-by-one-inch wood the width of the shelf minus three-quarters of an inch (the actual size of one-inch wood) and one strip the length of the shelf.
3. Mark the wall where you want the shelf to hang. Don't forget to take into account the thickness of the wood.
4. Check to make sure the marks are level.
5. Screw the one-by-ones to the wall, starting with the long strip for the back of the shelf first.
6. Add the two ends, then place the shelf on top.
7. Attach it with screws at about every six or eight inches to the wooden strips underneath.

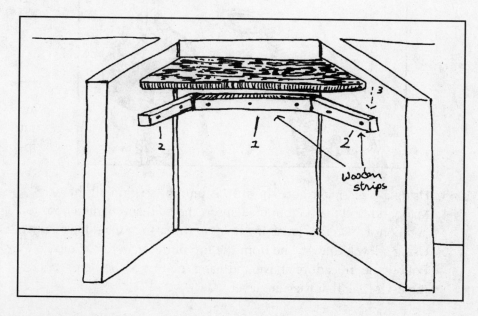

Metal Brackets

If the shelves are going to carry a heavy load, you should attach them directly to the wall studs. If this isn't possible, use toggle bolts. Most metal strips have a top and a bottom, so check yours first and put a piece of masking tape on the bottom end.

1. Place the strip against the wall where you want it to go and mark the wall where the top, predrilled hole is.
2. Drill the top hole only; insert the bolt but don't tighten it.

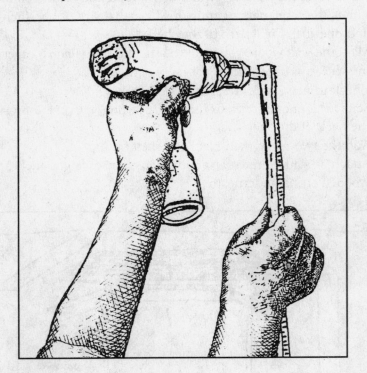

3. Using a level, make sure the strip is plumb (straight all the way).
4. Mark and drill the bottom hole, insert the bolt, and tighten both top and bottom. Do the remaining holes in the strip in the same manner.
5. Using a level, draw a line from the top of the strip to the next one. Follow the procedure above and hang the rest of the strips, checking each time that they are level.

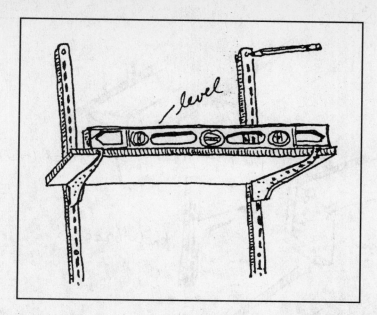

6. Insert the brackets. The shelf will be even more secure if it is bolted to the bracket, so most have holes designed for this purpose.

L Brackets

1. Mark the position where you want the bracket on the wall.
2. Using a carpenter's square and a level, mark the next bracket. Do all the brackets for one shelf before moving on to the next shelf.
3. Double-check that they are level, then mark the positions of all the rest of the brackets. It will be easier to drill all the holes at once instead of working around a bracket sticking out in your face.
4. Attach the brackets to the wall, one shelf at a time. Then, before moving on to the next, bolt the shelf to the bracket. Again, it will be easier to work without having to dodge an obstacle course of previously inserted brackets.

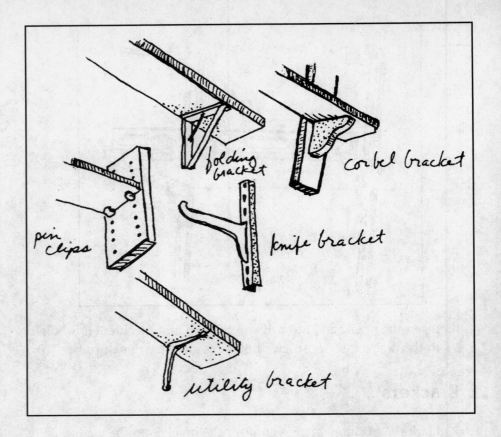

folding bracket

corbel bracket

pin clips

knife bracket

utility bracket

AND THE TEST ON THURSDAY WILL COVER . . .

With these techniques we've gone over the critical stuff:

1. Attaching things to the wall, properly
2. Making sure things are level
3. Securing the shelf to its support

You should now be able to adapt any attached shelving system to your needs. In the projects chapter, we will show you how to make a free-standing bookcase as well.

TAKE FIVE

See, we told you that drilling would be a snap. And, once you have the right attachments, almost any job will become a lot easier than if you did it manually. Most women we talked with said that they felt a little intimidated by drills—and these are the same women who handle electric curling irons, electronic depilatators, and Cuisinarts without blinking an eye. In reality, handling a drill is no more difficult than any of these appliances and, since you're not actually going to be applying it directly to any part of your body . . . well, you figure it out.

8

I'd Rather Lay a Tile

INSTALLING, REPAIRING, AND REPLACING VINYL AND CERAMIC TILE

Picture this: You've just spent the past twenty minutes relaxing in a hot bath filled with an intoxicating mixture of oils and perfumes. All of your tensions have melted away and are about to disappear down the drain, forever. You stand up, reach for a fluffy towel, and wrap it around yourself, lovingly. Now, you lift your foot out of the bath and place it on . . . the rough, naked wood that is on your bathroom floor. Now, what is wrong with this picture?

In this chapter, we will take you through the wonderful world of tile and show you how to replace, repair, and install wall and floor tile. We will start with a discussion about the different types of floor tile, vinyl and ceramic, and then finish up with a how-to on wall tile, which is usually only ceramic. If you're putting vinyl on your wall, we don't want to know about it. While we're at it, we will also give you some hints on how to use tile as a decorating aid and where you can get some really nifty tiles, as well.

FLOOR TILES

Sometimes, the houses and apartments we move into have tile floors that are less than OK. You know the kind we mean—tile that looks so old and cracked you expect to hear the theme song from the Addams Family play whenever you walk into the room. One of the ways you can really personalize and improve your home is by repairing or replacing the tile whether it be on the floor or on the walls. If, however, you are planning on laying down carpet or sheet vinyl, we would suggest that you use the services of a professional installer for the best results. In this chapter we are only going to deal with the installation and repair of vinyl, cork, and ceramic tiles, a job that if you are patient and meticulous, you really can accomplish yourself.

Choosing the Tile

The first thing you will need to decide is what kind of tile you want to use, **vinyl (synthetic or natural linoleum)**, **cork**, or **ceramic**. Don't wrinkle up your face when we mention vinyl . . . we're not talking about that old black-and-white stuff that used to cover your mother's kitchen floor. Vinyl tiles have come of age and are now as attractive and versatile as any ceramic tile but cost a whole lost less. The quality and price are as varied as the patterns they come in, so we're sure you can find something to suit your needs. Vinyl tiles are also fairly easy to apply and come in both **self-adhesive** forms as well as those to which you need to **apply an adhesive**. Vinyl and cork tiles are almost always twelve-inch squares (that is, one square foot), whereas ceramic tile comes in many different sizes and shapes.

Tip #1: Just a Little Taste

If you're not sure how you will like the color or pattern you have chosen, buy about half a dozen of each pattern you like, lay them out without taking the backing off, and stand back and observe. Unless they are special-ordered, you can always bring back the ones you don't like.

Ceramic tiles are much more expensive but if the rich effect is what your heart desires and you can swing it, go for it. With ceramic tiles, you get to choose not only the color you like but also the shape, size, and finish (glazed, unglazed, or matte finish) as well. The fun of using ceramic tiles is that you get to mix and match the different tiles and, after adding whatever color grout you like, end up with your own personalized mosaic.

On the downside, ceramic tiles are harder to apply than vinyl or cork. They're more difficult to cut, and installation requires a few additional steps, such as mixing and applying a mortar and grouting, then letting the whole thing set for a week afterwards. You also need to make sure that your floor will support the added weight of ceramic tile. This is an especially important consideration for apartment and condo dwellers.

When choosing your tile, there are several things you need to keep in mind. Ceramic tiles are rated according to their permeability; i.e., how much water they will absorb. There are four classifications ranging from *nonvitreous,* the most absorbent, to *semivitreous, vitreous*, and finally, *impervious*, the kind that can withstand water the best. The type you choose will depend on where you want to use it. For example, since an unglazed terra-cotta tile is nonvitreous and soaks up water easily, you would not want to install it in a bathroom where there is apt to be a lot of water. Ceramic tile or another vitreous or impervious tile would be the better choice.

Tiles also come in different thicknesses, with wall tiles being thinner and not as strong as floor tiles. Make sure to use floor tiles on surfaces where you will be walking or putting down heavy objects, since the thinner tiles will not withstand the additional stress and weight put on them.

Cork tiles have come a long way since the days of lava lamps and the kind of cork walls that looked like giant moth-eaten, crumbling bulletin boards. They now come prefinished with wax, polyurethane, or even vinyl coated, in everything from a soft matte to a lustrous, sophisticated high-gloss finish. The color range tends to be in the brown family and the price is a bit more than vinyl, but less than ceramic tiles so it might be a way to individualize your look for not a lot of money. Cork is easy to install, soft underfoot, cleans easily, and can even help insulate your floors. Not to beat a dead horse here, but since cork comes from the bark of trees, it's a renewable resource, too.

How Much Is Too Much? . . . Determining How Much Tile You Need

In order to figure out how many you will need, you first have to calculate the square footage of the space you want to tile. That, for those of you who remember your high-school math, is accomplished by multiplying the length of the room by the width. The resulting measure will give you the number of whole squares you will need. Please be aware that there will be some areas left over in which you will have to lay partial tiles, so buy enough extra material. Also, since cork and natural linoleum are natural products, different lots will vary in color, so try to buy all the tile at once, and if possible, make sure you can return any leftovers.

Tip #2: Leveling the Playing Field

Whether you are using vinyl, cork, or ceramic tile, there are two important things to keep in mind: the floor must be clean and level, and you need to decide where you start your tile.

Installing Vinyl Tiles

PREPARING THE FLOOR

In most cases, vinyl tile can be laid over concrete or wood. If you have a concrete floor laid directly on the soil beneath, check before you buy tile since some types of vinyl will not work in this situation. A few tiles can be laid over other resilient flooring, but in most cases, there's no getting around it—you will need to pull up the old vinyl. Whatever the surface you find underneath, it must be clean, dry, and level. Pull up any glue or rubber backing, nail down loose nails, and, in general, get rid of any debris. You will need to fill in any cracks or gouges that you find with wood filler.

Pry off the baseboard and remove any carpet strips. Using a **pry bar**, gently pull the board away from the wall. Don't attack it or try to force it all up at once. You're not looking to impress anyone, here, so just work your way gradually along the board, taking care that it doesn't split. Think of doing it in the same way you would pry the lid off a can of paint: start at one point, push it up a bit, then work your way all around the lid. When you get back to the starting point, you're home free and you can pry it all the way off.

If the floor you find underneath looks as though some underground creatures have been partying hardy, you should cover it with a layer of **one-quarter-inch plywood** or any similar material. Have the lumberyard cut the sheets in half for easier handling. Incidentally, since a four-by-eight-inch sheet of plywood is way too heavy and bulky for one person to handle alone, this might be one of those times when you tempt your significant other into lending you a hand. A bottle of champagne will make even a job like this seem like fun.

Now, starting in the center of the room, **lay out** the four-by-eight sheets with their seams staggered, as illustrated below. Put down all the whole pieces you can first, then **adjust** if needed. For example, if you find you have a three-inch gap at one end and a fifteen-inch one at the other end, you may want to slide the whole thing to one end so you only have one side to piece instead of two.

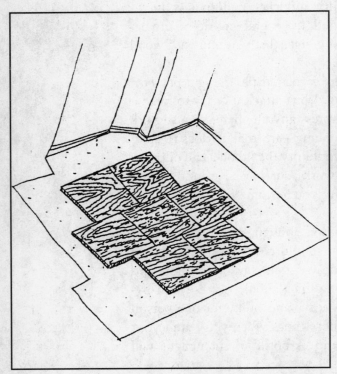 

Nail the plywood down with **ring shank flooring nails**. Using a long straightedge, measure and cut boards to fit any remaining gaps and nail those into place. Leave the baseboards off until after you've laid the tile.

Concrete floors should be checked with a long straightedge to see if they are level. To do this, hold the edge perpendicular to the floor and then, as you move it across the floor, watch for gaps between the two surfaces. (If you feel like an old miner working with a divining rod, you're doing it properly.)

Fill in any depressions with latex or vinyl cement. After the cement has dried, sand it smooth and then double-check to see if your repairs worked. Take the time to do this part of the job right. No cheating allowed because the tile simply will not lie properly if the floor isn't level.

If your floor currently has old ceramic tile on it, you will have to remove it. This process can be a bit tedious, so be forewarned. You will need to use a **chisel** and **hammer** to pry off the first tile. Since a good way to go about doing this is to smash down on the first tile, this could be a good way to work off some of the aggression that built up when your mother reminded you that, by your age, she already had two children with one more on the way. Just picture that "I feel so sorry for you" smile she had on her face and smash away!

Take a **bolster chisel** which has a wider blade than a regular chisel and work your way underneath each tile. When you have lifted them all up and off, chop away any remaining mortar and smooth out the floor. By the way, you should definitely wear safety goggles while doing this as tile tends to shatter into lots of eye-splintering pieces.

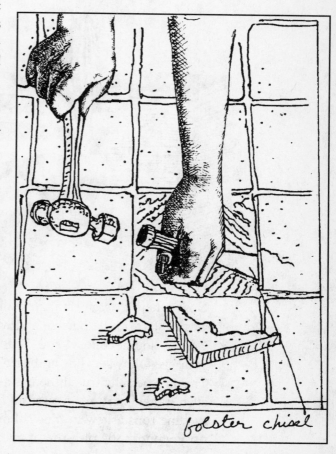

bolster chisel

Now, where do you think you should lay your first tile? If your answer was to start on the outside and work your way in, you lose. Do not pass Go and do not collect $200. The idea behind laying tile is to do it so that your eye follows its line and isn't drawn to any irregularities in the room. This is especially true if there is a pattern in the tile you have chosen. But even if there isn't one, you want the effect to be sweeping, not choppy. If the line runs askew to the wall or cabinetry, it will make you feel a little tipsy without the pleasure of imbibing—and that's no fun at all.

Stand in the doorway and get a good look at your room. Note where your eye goes naturally. Do you have a row of cabinets that dominates the room, or is there a door you catch sight of first? It might help to make a sketch of the room and note these features. Then measure everything, write it on the drawing, and measure again, just to make sure.

The size of the tile will determine how you go from here. Although vinyl tiles come in twelve-inch squares, it is unlikely that your room will form a perfect square. Therefore, you will probably need to use some *partial* tiles as well as the full ones. You must determine at which end of the room they will be less obvious once they are laid.

Tip #4: Like a Giant Puzzle

Although many recommend starting in the exact middle of your room, we have found that, if you do it that way, the tile will take the lead and you'll end up like a mouse in a maze, with no control over where you can put the cut tiles. We advise that you find the center of the room and then, depending on where you want the partial tile to end up, move the starting point to one side or the other.

By the way, since walls are rarely set in perfect right angles, if you start in the center of the room rather than in the corner, you will be able to spread the differences in the shapes of the cut tiles in all directions, making them less easy to spot.

Where's Copernicus When You Really Need Him? Finding the Center of the Room

Measure wall A; determine the exact center. **Measure wall B**; determine its exact center. Don't assume it is the same as A, even if it looks similar. **Snap a chalk line** (1) between the two. **Mark the center** of (1) and, using a carpenter's square, **draw a line** (2) at exactly ninety degrees to the first chalk line. If your room is large enough, double-check this by marking a point **three feet** out on line (2). Mark a point **four feet** out on line (1). **Measure**

the distance between these two points. It should be exactly *five feet* if the angle is at ninety degrees. If it's not, start over as it is absolutely critical to get this right or the tiles will be crooked.

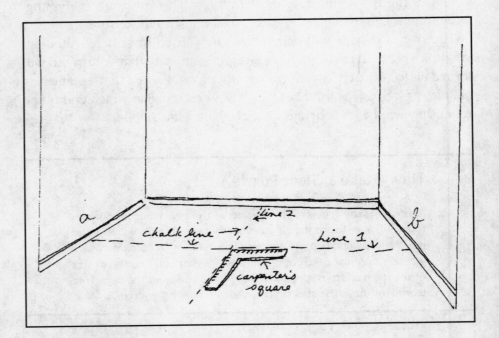

This same formula of *"three, four, and five"* applies to any unit of measurement: feet, inches, meters, etc.

Tip #5: Odd Room Out

If your room is oddly shaped, you need to find its focal point (a fireplace, bay window, door, etc.) and center the lines indicated above in front of that.

GETTING LAID . . . TILE PLACEMENT

Now, for the fun part. If you were good at playing blocks when you were a kid, this should be a breeze. If you got frustrated easily, you might have the same trouble here. Try not to cry and stomp your feet, though, or you'll jostle the tile.

General Guidelines

Lay a dry run of the tile using the following guidelines:

1. **For a border or strong pattern:** Center the tiles, leaving the same-size cut tiles on opposite edges.
2. **No pattern:** Move the starting point so you have a line of whole tiles along two sides. Try to cut as few tiles as possible. It's less wasteful and a lot easier.
3. **By the entranceway:** Do not use cut pieces near the entrance since they will be the first things you see as you enter the room.
4. **Borders and irregular shapes:** To get a fit at the border, place a tile upside down exactly on top of the last full tile. Place another tile on top, but touching the wall. Draw a line along the edge of this tile on the backside of the tile. Cut the tile with a utility knife and a straightedge, then press in place.

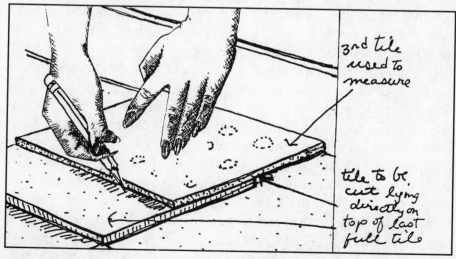

5. To cut around awkward curves you can take a piece of paper and press it around the curve, revealing the shape. Cut along the crease and use it as a pattern.

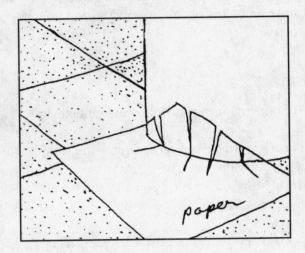

SELF-ADHESIVE VINYL TILES

After you buy your tiles, as you did with the wood, let them sit in the room for twenty-four hours to acclimatize. Check the back of the tile to see if there are any arrows indicating a directional pattern. If there are, make sure you lay them all pointing in the same direction.

Starting at the center point of the tile, peel the backing off and carefully place it at the juncture of lines (1) and (2). Make sure the tile follows the chalk lines. Lay the next tile at the juncture on the other side of the chalk lines. Place the second tile firmly against the edge of the first one and, as you lay it, push against the first tile so they are as close together as possible. You will find that it is extremely hard to pull up the tiles without damaging them, so work carefully. (If you do make a serious mistake, however, you will have to pull it up and replace it.)

Lay the next tile directly above the first, again following the chalk line. Lay the next one above the second tile to make a square. Working out from both sides, form the shape of a pyramid. Continue until half the room is finished, then turn around and repeat this process on the other side. Let sit for twenty-four hours before mopping.

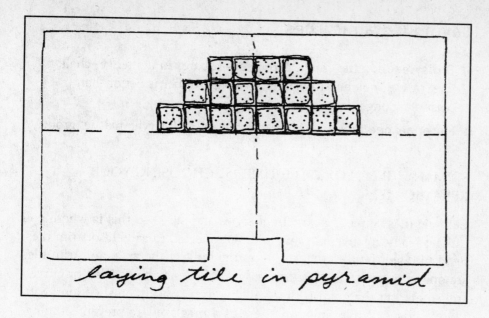

laying tile in pyramid

NON-SELF-ADHESIVE VINYL TILES

Follow the manufacturer's directions when buying your adhesive so you make sure you get the kind that will allow the tiles you bought to stick. Prepare the adhesive using a three-sixteenth-inch notched spreader and then spread enough adhesive for two or three tiles at a time. Set the tiles and wipe off any excess adhesive *immediately* with a damp rag. When they are ready, set them in the same manner as is indicated above for the self-adhesive tiles.

When the floor is completed, wipe it with a damp rag to remove any marks but do not mop it for at least twenty-four hours.

Finish the floor by renailing the baseboards into place and adding a metal carpet strip at the doorway.

Tip #6: Damn, I Just Chipped My Tile

If you have to replace a damaged vinyl tile, try chiseling it out from the center. Use pliers to get a better grip on the pieces. If you have difficulty, use an iron to warm and soften the adhesive and it should lift out easily.

Laying Ceramic Tiles

Tools needed: tile cutter, carpenter's square, straightedge, chalk line, trowel, notched trowel, grout float (rubber is better than plastic), sponges

Materials needed: tiles, spacers, thin set and acrylic mastic, grout

SO MANY TILES, SO LITTLE TIME . . . CHOOSING YOUR CERAMIC TILES

Ceramic tiles come in a variety of styles and sizes, so this is where you can get really creative. Ceramic tiles are referred to as field or trim tiles. Field tiles are the tiles that make up the bulk of the area, and trim tiles are ones you use to finish off the edges. They may be beveled or curved and so on, but the point is they will give you a nicely finished look with smooth edges. While almost all these tiles are glazed, to prevent slipping, floor tiles are not as highly glazed as wall tiles. *Quarry tiles* have no glaze at all and will need to be sealed after you install them.

Tip #7: Taking a Soak

Soak quarry tiles in water before laying them. This way they won't suck all the moisture out of the mastic before they cure properly.

Mosaic tiles are smaller than the loose tiles and come in sheets from six by twelve inches to twelve by twenty-four inches. The mosaics are attached to a strip of *nonremovable* plastic mesh so that they stay evenly spaced and can be applied easily or are face mounted, which means that they have a paper on top of them to protect their finish. When you are ready to set the face-mounted tiles, you lay their backs in the adhesive, dampen the paper, and then, after the adhesive has set but before you do the grouting, pull the paper away. Mosaic tiles are easy to apply as borders either alone or in combination with loose tiles.

Joan used to live next door to a man, a doctor, who made tables out of mosaic tiles. For hour after hour he would sit handling the tiny pieces and laying them out in one intricate pattern after another. They say that tile laying and bead stringing are the most popular activities in mental hospitals—kind of makes you wonder, doesn't it?

There are also some **specialty tiles**, such as inside and outside corner tiles and marble saddles, that you can use as sills in door thresholds and tiles that can serve as baseboards, which are known as cove bases. You buy these by the piece when you have a specific need for them.

DOING THE DEED . . . PLACING CERAMIC TILE

In laying down ceramic tiles, the basic floor preparation is exactly the same as for vinyl. Likewise for finding the center of the room. There are, however, two schools of thought about where to start with ceramic tiles:

1. Find the center of your room and determine the starting point as you would for vinyl tiles.
2. Or, start in a corner at the line where the last row of complete tiles would be. In this case you would make a perfect ninety-degree triangle using the three, four, five ratio just as you do when you start in the center, then work your way out from the corner.

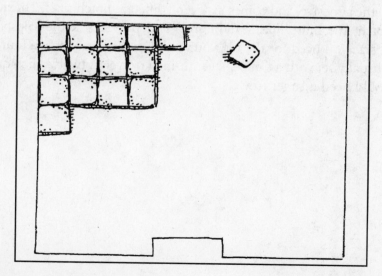

In either case, you will have to take more care than you did with vinyl tiles in terms of where you place the cut tiles. Cut ceramic tile edges are very sharp, and not only will they look bad if they are in your entranceway but they might also cut the feet of your visitors and loved ones, leaving you liable for a whopping big lawsuit. Just remember, you were warned.

Tip #8: Up Against the Wall!

If you are tiling a bathroom floor, it will look better if the tiles that are up against the tub or shower are complete and uncut.

When comparing vinyl and ceramic tiles, the major difference in appearance and application has to do with the spacing between the tiles. With vinyl, tiles are laid next to one another with no separation. With ceramic, you must leave space for the grout to be added.

Spacers are small plastic or wood inserts that you use between the tiles to temporarily maintain even grout joints. These come in sizes from one-sixteenth of an inch to one-quarter inch. When you choose your tile think about the look you want and buy spacers accordingly. You'll need several dozen at least. A *trowel* is a flat tool with a handle that is used to spread the adhesive, and comes in several different notch sizes. The deeper the notch, the more mastic (adhesive) it deposits. Ask the salesperson which size you need for the tile you've chosen. For instance, a four-inch tile is usually set with a three-sixteenth-inch trowel. A twelve-inch quarry tile would need a larger trowel.

Tip #9: Follow That Line

If, when you are laying out the ceramic tiles, it seems that it will be hard to follow the chalk lines accurately, you can nail a long piece of wood along the lines and use it to keep the tiles straight. If you do this, include spacers and double-check that you haven't shifted anything while nailing the wood down. If you have, adjust your center starting point accordingly.

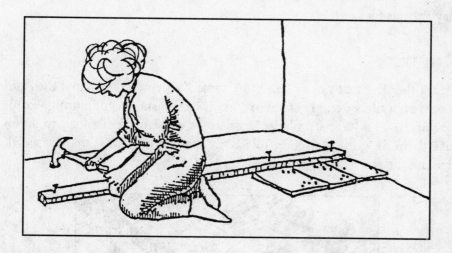

MIXING THE MORTAR

Mix a batch of **thin set mortar** with the **acrylic mastic**. While you can just use thin set mortar mixed with water, it will be far stronger if mixed with the acrylic. Hold the trowel at a forty-five-degree angle and start by spreading the mixture on an area of about two feet by two feet. Remember not to cover up your chalk lines. As you build up your experience and comfort level, you can increase the size of the area—but don't get too far ahead or it'll dry out.

WHOLE TILES

Lay the first tile in the corner of the right angle, then form a square around it. Wipe off any excess mortar that gets on the tiles with a damp sponge. Work your way across the floor until the room is finished except for the borders of cut tiles. Don't walk on newly laid tiles unless you absolutely have to. If you do, lay a smooth piece of plywood over the tiles, making sure you don't scratch the tile.

Let the tiles set for twenty-four hours before you walk on them, then lay the cut tiles.

CUT TILES

Mark the tiles that need cutting the same way you would vinyl tiles and cut with a tile cutter. There aren't any tricks to successful cutting except for practice and a sharp blade. Most stores will cut the tile for you if you ask them. In our experience, this is the hardest part, so it may be worth having the store do it for you.

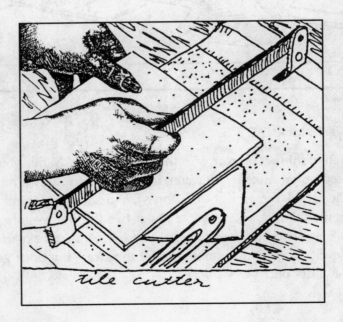

tile cutter

Set cut pieces in place as you did the whole tiles. If you've taken the baseboards off, any slightly crooked edges that appear on the cut pieces won't show after they're replaced. Set the borders and let dry. Remove the spacers.

GROUTING

If your tiles are glazed, you can grout them at this point. If, however, they are not (as with quarry tiles), you must seal them first. Sealing is a must or else they will become stained easily. Follow the manufacturer's directions on the sealing product and then let them dry for the recommended time.

Tip #10: Something to Grout About

There are two kinds of grout, sanded or nonsanded. If your tiles are spaced up to one-eighth inch apart, use nonsanded grout, if more than one-eighth inch apart, use sanded grout.

Mix up a batch of grout according to the manufacturer's instructions. You will use an item known as a **float**. This looks like a trowel except it is thicker and lighter and is used for spreading the grout. The best kind to get is a rubber grout float (just try saying that three times without stopping). It is a little more expensive than the plastic ones but works better because it leaves less grout behind on the tiles to clean up afterwards.

Place a dollop of grout on your float, holding it at a forty-five-degree angle, then spread the grout in a horizontal line across the tiles. Make sure you have packed the grout in the spaces, leaving no gaps. Wipe the excess grout off the tiles before it dries.

 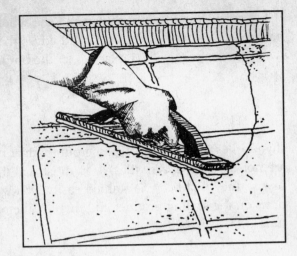

Let dry for six or seven days, then seal the grout using a small brush dipped in sealant. It will probably take two or three coats.

Tip #11: Variety Is the Spice of Life

Following are a few decorator tips we got from the pros on laying ceramic tiles:

1. Lay the tile diagonally.
2. Create a border or pattern with a different tile.
3. Buy a few more expensive tiles to lay in the midst of your loose tiles. You can find some amazing tiles that, in bulk, are too expensive for an entire floor but are affordable in a smaller quantity.
4. Haunt flea markets for the occasional deco or country antique tile. If you are not sure of their durability, however, it might be better to use them on a wall rather than on the floor. Joan got some real beauties which she mounted on the wall and used for trivets, too.

DON'T GO BREAKING MY HEART . . . REPLACING A BROKEN CERAMIC TILE

If you find that one of the tiles you put in broke or if you need to replace a tile in your existing floor, try the following:

1. Chisel out the grout around the tile.
2. Tap tile with a hammer to break it, then pry it up.
3. Remove as much mortar as possible, then set new tile in fresh mortar.
4. Let dry and grout as above.

Tip #12: Before Our Time

Tile made before the 1960s was often set in a masonry base, which makes its removal much more difficult. We suggest getting a professional to do your repairs in older tile.

GET THE GROUT OUT OF HERE . . . RENOVATING GROUT

Sometimes, all your floor needs is a clean coat of grout. Think of it like adding highlights instead of changing your entire hair color.

First, clean out any of the old, crumbly stuff which is there now. Then, mix up a batch of fresh grout and apply as we described above. Make sure you force the new grout into the crevices so that there are no gaps. Let dry and seal as usual.

Tip #13: So You Want to Be a Bottle Blond

If your old grout is in good shape but is discolored, you can clean it with bleach or with **"White'N Brite,"** a phosphoric acid–based product. In both cases you'll need to scrub with something like a toothbrush to really get it clean before you apply the product. A little warning: Both products give off nasty fumes, so remember to ventilate.

TILING THE WALLS

We're going to assume that no one is interested in tiling her walls with vinyl since we're not really big into tacky, so we'll just deal with ceramic tile. As we mentioned earlier, wall tiles are thinner and lighter than floor tiles. They also, almost always, come with small bumps on their bottom edges which act like built-in spacers and make applying them a little easier. However, tiling a wall that has fixtures like soap dishes, toothpaste holders, etc., is slightly more tedious than tiling a floor since it requires more cutting and planning, so you come out about even.

Wall, Are You Ready for This? . . . Preparing the Wall

Since tile cannot be laid over wallpaper, peeling paint, or uneven surfaces, you might need to look back at the painting chapter to refresh your memory about how to prepare your walls. In some cases wallpaper can be laid over existing tile, but we don't recommend it.

Tile also cannot be laid directly over Sheetrock since Sheetrock is gypsum sandwiched between paper. In other words, if it gets wet from the moisture in the mortar, it's Crumble City, all the way. The best thing to do if you have Sheetrock on your wall is to put up one-quarter-inch **green board** as a moisture barrier. You can also use a special paper available at the hardware store as a moisture barrier.

The Layout

Once you have prepared your walls, you need to make sure the layout you have planned will work. If the entire wall is plain and unadorned, no sweat. If, however, your wall is against a sink or a shower stall or contains fixtures, you'll need to take into account any kind of special edging tiles needed. Measure carefully, remembering to include the spacing for the grout.

wall

level

guide/support board

Tip #14: Only Anal Retentives Need Apply

An easy way to ensure that your measurements stay accurate is by making a gauge stick. Lay out eight to ten tiles with any spacers needed. Place a one-by-two-inch-wide and three-to-four-foot-long wooden strip against the tiles and mark off the spaces indicated. This will help determine the layout and keep it even as you work.

Mark the bottom row of uncut tiles and measure up to the last row of uncut tiles at the top. If the remaining row of cut tiles is very narrow, adjust up or down as necessary. The principle here is the same as for the floor: you want to avoid a too-narrow border so, if both sides of a wall are visible, your borders should be approximately equal.

Once you have determined the placement of the bottom row of uncut tiles, it's helpful to nail a thin piece of wood to the wall as a guide and to support the weight of the tiles. Check that the wood guide is even by using at least a two-foot level. Don't rely on a six-inch one for this since it is too easy to be off and you'll just end up with a whole mess of crooked tiles. Run a chalk line at ninety degrees to the baseline to the point where the last vertical row of uncut tiles will be. Nailing in another thin board as a guide along this line may be helpful, too.

The Application

Beginning in the corner, spread mastic over a two-foot-square area and begin setting tile. Use spacers if needed, but the bottom bumpers should work. Be careful you don't slide tiles into place. It's better to position them close to where you want them and then set them with a little twist—it's kind of like adding a twist to a martini. Wipe off any excess mastic as you go.

Once all the uncut tiles are in place, it's time for the tedious business of trimming tiles for the borders and to go around pipes and fixtures. Measure the distance between the top row of tiles and the wall. Then measure the distance between the bottom row and the wall. If the two numbers are equal or almost equal, you can cut all the tiles at once without having to measure each space individually. If not, you're out of luck and you'll need to work your way down the wall, measuring as you go.

When you're finally done, set the little tile tidbits in place, add any of the finishing touches like a soap dish, and let cure for twenty-four hours. In order to keep soap dishes and other accessories from sliding around while curing, tape them to the surrounding tiles with masking tape.

It's Grouting Time Again

Prepare the grout as you did for the floor tile but make sure that you use a rubber float. Hold the float at a forty-five-degree angle and spread the grout in a diagonal line across the tiles. Make sure it's packed into all the spaces, then wipe it off the tiles before it dries. By the way, if you are tiling a shower or anyplace that water might reach, the grout must be waterproof. You can also buy a grout with a mildew-cide in it.

Some people recommend smoothing the joints for a finished look. You can use a small wooden dowel or the handle of a toothbrush for this. Clean the tiles gently, taking care not to disturb the grout.

Let dry for six to seven days and then seal as you did with the floor.

Caulking

Before you sign off on your bathroom walls, you will need to run a line of caulk around all the joints, wherever the tile joins the tub, door, toilet, window, or anything else that is not tile. If you use grout around these points, it will crack as it expands or contracts, whereas caulk is flexible enough not to crack.

Caulk is silicone based, comes in a tube you squeeze out like toothpaste, and can be bought in a variety of colors to match your grout. When you first open the tube, be careful that you don't make the hole too wide or else too much caulk will come pouring out. You want to match the size of the hole to the width of the space that needs to be filled.

Prepare the space to be caulked by cleaning away any debris or leftover adhesive with a cloth that you have moistened in denatured alcohol. Then place the tip of the caulking tube at a forty-five-degree angle to the crack line and gently draw it toward you. It's a little bit like the technique you use when you are finishing off a cake with decorative icing. When you finish the row, lift the tip of the tube up with a gentle twisting action. To finish it off, wet your finger with the alcohol and lightly run it along the caulk line to smooth it and force the caulk deeper into the crack.

You can also apply caulk with a caulking gun. You attach the tube to the gun, then use the trigger to force the caulk out.

Tip #17: Rub a Dub Dub

When you caulk around your bathtub, it is a good idea to fill the tub with water first. The weight of the water will make the tub pull away from the wall, and you will be able to see the separation you need to fill. When the tub is empty again, it will rise up ever so slightly and, automatically, press the caulk deeper into the joints.

If you have removed your wall fixtures while tiling, make sure you replace them using a glue specially made for installing fixtures. An epoxy-based glue should work, too, but don't use the same adhesive you used to apply the tiles as it will not hold it well enough.

When you have glued the fixtures back in place, put a few layers of masking tape on them to hold them down until the glue has set. It might take a few days, so resist the urge to peek.

Tip #18: You Can Count on It

If you want to tile your kitchen counter, you do it exactly the same way as you did the walls—with one big difference: Use an epoxy-based grout to help keep the surface germ free.

TAKE FIVE

Looking back, this might seem like a really big project, but the rewards of having tiled your own bathroom or kitchen are great as well as money saving. We don't know about you, but we think spending time alone in a luxurious bath is one of the greatest pleasures a woman can have. So, while some of the repairs you will do around the house are to be shared by others, this one is for you and you alone.

CHAPTER

It's Better Than Collagen

FURNITURE REFINISHING

Hey, do you remember that tacky old table your grandmother kept in the foyer of her house? You know, the one that looked as if she had carted it all the way from Russia with her that she promised would one day be yours? (At the time, you probably thought something akin to "when donkeys fly," right?). Well, doesn't Grandma's old table look exactly like the one *you* carted home from that antiques fair last Saturday?

Alas, it's true . . . yesterday's junk has become today's flea market find. The question is, What do you do with it once it's home and you see exactly how moth-eaten and worm rotten it really is? In this chapter, we will take you through the steps of how to turn your weekend booty into a real prize. You will also be able to give a new look to an old favorite you already have and learn how to keep your furniture from showing the wear and tear of time, as well. Ah, if only we could do the same things for our faces and bodies—why, we wouldn't have had to write this book at all. We could have just patented our private fountain of youth and retired to Antigua. Well, the Caribbean's loss is your gain, so give us your tired, your poor, and we will help you find life after the attic.

There are, basically, three steps to follow in achieving your goal.

STRIPPING: removing old finishes or paints on the surface
REPAIRING: fixing holes or gouges in the wood
REFINISHING: applying a paint or stain and then a sealer to the wood

STRIPPING

Materials needed: sandpaper, gloves, drop cloth, rags, soluble stripper, paint thinner

Tools needed: paintbrushes, putty knife, electric sander (optional)

Apologies to Demi Moore, but **stripping** is the process of removing anything that is currently covering the surface of the wood. You'll want to do it if a piece of furniture has been covered over with many layers of paint or if you just want to remove the varnish covering the wood. The three most usual methods you can use are **sanding (hand or electric),** *heat stripping*, and *chemical stripping*. Usually you use sanding and scraping as the first steps in removing your finish and then again at the end before you are ready to refinish it. For pieces that are too delicate to be heat or chemical stripped, sanding is the best and only way to strip but, for others, you will need to take additional steps. Please note that in this chapter we will refer to two different types of sanding: one for *removing an old finish* and the other for *finish-sanding*. Both employ slightly different techniques. In this section, we are describing the kind of sanding you do to remove a finish. (That kind of sounded like a Gracie Allen explanation, but we're sure you got the picture.)

As we told you in the chapter on painting, the whole stripping process can be very, very messy, and you will be working with some pretty strong chemicals. So make sure that you set yourself up in a well-ventilated area. It's probably a good idea to put one of those terribly attractive white masks over your face to protect you from inhaling too much of the fumes from the solvent. If you can work outside, all the better as the fumes from any strippers are very unhealthy. Gloves are a definite must.

Before you start, make sure that you lay out a drop cloth or cover your floor with several layers of newspaper. You will also want to remove all the hinges, knobs, or any other metal hardware that is attached to the furniture and clean them thoroughly.

Hand Sanding

Real furniture refinishers still feel that **hand sanding** is the *only* way to strip furniture and still preserve the integrity of the wood, along with any intricacies in the woodworking. With hand sanding you have better control of what you are doing and you can really get into corners and irregular shapes without fear of damage. It is slow and painstaking, however, so choose this method only if you've got the time for it.

As with most of the tasks we have described, the preparatory work here is essential to achieving a good final result. Sanding is, therefore, very important. You will want to have several different grades of sandpaper on hand as the more coarse papers are better for removing large areas of paint, but once you have gotten most of that off, you will want to use a finer-textured paper for smoothing.

Tip #1: Sandy Side Up

You will do better with hand sanding if you take each piece of sandpaper and cut it into smaller pieces, usually in fourths, before you use it. It will make the pieces last longer and be less likely to tear than if you used the whole piece.

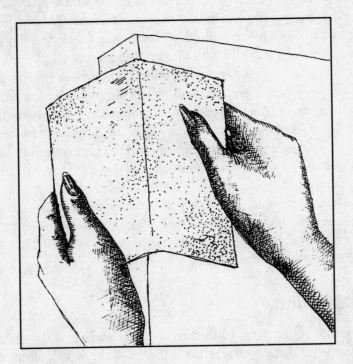

Before you start, take one end of the paper in each hand and then, with the smooth side down, pull it over an edge. Turn it slightly to the right and repeat. This makes the paper more flexible so you can handle it more easily.

You can also use fine-grade steel wool to finish the piece. It's easier to get in crevices with steel wool than with sandpaper. Remember that any little flecks of paint you leave will turn up as bumps under the surface you are going to apply.

A *sanding cord* is a string that, like sandpaper, comes in several different grits. It is excellent for getting into the kinds of knobs and crevices one might find on rocking chairs and around the decorative accents found on bedposts and other chair backs. (You use it exactly the way you'd floss your teeth.)

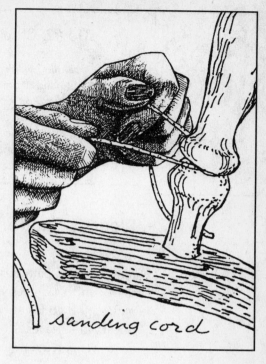

sanding cord

Always make sure that you sand in the same direction as the wood grain and don't get too enthusiastic about what you are doing or else you might change the color of the wood, lower the whole level of the surface by as much as an inch, and, in general, damage carvings, patina, and edges. So, check the wood as you go along and, as with all things in life, know when to stop.

When you have reached the naked wood, run a piece of cloth over the surface to remove any leftover pieces of wood as well as the debris from the sandpaper. In order to really make sure that the wood is ready for the next phase, take a pair of panty hose and run it all over the surface. If it snags, you have to go back and do it again. By the way, we hope you realize that we meant for you to use an old pair of panty hose. We don't care how strong those L'Eggs are supposed to be, this is not the way to test them.

teardrop sander

Tip #2: Chip off the Old Block

A **sanding block** is a device to help you hand sand that can save your hands from unsightly blisters and calluses as well as ward off splinters. For those of you who have been afraid of applying too much pressure on your sandpaper, this method is ideal as it will let you really dig in.

A teardrop-shaped sanding block lets you sand around contours or strangely shaped areas.

Electric Sanders

In the chapter on how to paint, we discussed electric sanders as a way of removing old paint from a surface. We had some concerns about their use there, and that goes double here. While electric sanders will definitely make a job go faster, we cannot recommend them except for use on flat, uncarved surfaces. Don't use them on any antique furniture, especially if it was veneered, or on anything that has a detailed or carved surface. Save them for when you are sanding a wood floor or any other wood surface that is plain and large in area.

That having been said, two of them could come in handy for specific purposes:

Belt sanders can be useful for tabletops and other larger flat surfaces. Be careful when going around edges or anything curved, however. Also, watch out for the belt sander's tendency to eat away at the patina of the wood and leave irregular surfaces. Stain will not adhere evenly to surfaces with ridges and dents. (Think of it like makeup on blemished skin.) Make sure you do not hold the belt sander in one place for too long. It's better to keep it moving all the time so that grooves do not develop beneath the surface.

Orbital sanders are slightly better when it comes to preserving the surface, but they often work so quickly that a corner can be rounded and a carving flattened out before you even notice.

Chemical Stripping

The type of stripping solvent you will use is determined by the type of finish currently on your wood. Always check the instructions on the can in the store before you buy it. If you use the wrong kind, you could damage your furniture before you even get started. If your furniture has a grooved or vertical surface, you should use a heavy-bodied product. If, on the other hand, your piece has been covered over by an epoxy paint, a semipaste will do a better job.

Apply the solvent with a paintbrush. In the painting chapter we suggested that you get the best-quality brushes you can afford but here, the cheaper the better. The little sucker will never survive its encounter with the chemicals in the solvent, so no need to go crazy. You might want to apply solvent with those small foam sponges that come on a stick, too.

The directions on the container will tell you how long you need to leave the solvent on. Once the solvent is applied, you will notice that the paint on the furniture starts to bubble as the solvent eats its way through. (Just imagine what that could do to your skin if you weren't wearing gloves.) When the correct amount of time has passed, your paint should have acquired a somewhat squishy quality. Take your putty knife (the kind with a rounded edge, please) and start to remove the paint mush. You can also use a wood scraper but, whatever you do, please be careful. Don't attack the wood; think of tickling the paint off.

You might need to use another coat or two of the solvent, depending on how firmly attached the old paint was to the surface. When you have gotten all the large pieces of paint off, use an old toothbrush to go after the little specks that remain. Once again, easy but thoroughly does it. By the time you are finished, there should be no dark areas of paint remaining—the surface should be as clean as the proverbial baby's bottom.

Use a clean brush to go over the surface one more time with a paint thinner and then wipe all that off with a soft cloth. *Ta-da!*—as your mother used to say—it's so clean you could eat off it.

By the way, if you see paint on the hardware you removed earlier, just soak those items in some paint thinner for about ten minutes and then go after any offending specks that still remain with a piece of steel wool.

Heat Stripping

This is more for the daredevils out there. Those of you who have a fear of fire (Joan is leaving the room even as we speak), don't bother to read on. In reality there is no flame to be seen on a heat gun, just an extreme amount of heat. It's kind of like being in Phoenix in the middle of August.

Heat guns are good, however, for those people who have a real problem with the fumes given off by chemical strippers. We recommend using it only when removing paint finishes. Never use heat guns to remove veneer or on wood that is paneled. They are useful for speeding up the drying time of a stain or to get rid of old glue that is hiding out underneath the surface of an old veneer, but make sure you have them on a low setting before you start. The cost of a heat gun is an important factor in your decision to buy one. Although they can run between $50 to $80, once you have one you can save a lot down the road on the cost of chemical strippers.

These mothers heat up fast, by the way, and the air coming out of them can reach temperatures of 2,000 degrees in less than a minute. You will want to use a heat shield—in the form of a piece of heavy cardboard or aluminum foil—to protect the areas around where you are applying the heat.

When you turn the heat gun on, start at the lowest setting and work your way up. Hold it about two inches above the surface you want removed and move it around in a circular pattern. As the paint heats up, it will start to blister. Now, here is the tricky part: You have to move the gun out of the way and, using the other hand, advance with your paint scraper—pronto! If you wait too long, the paint will start to turn into a mushlike substance which will melt into the pores of the wood and damage it beneath the surface. If you get the timing of this right, you should be able to whisk away the dried-out paint with only a swipe of a piece of steel wool or a slice of the scraper while it is in its semihard, blistered state.

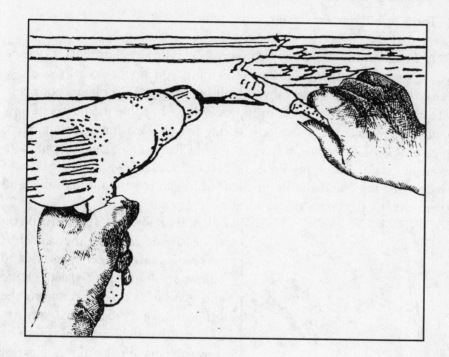

Tip #4: One, Two—Cha, Cha, Cha

The object is to develop a rhythm between the circular motion of the heat gun in one hand and the steady approach of the scraper in the other. If you can't master it, turn off the heat gun when you have softened a small portion of the paint and remove the paint with steel wool. The turn the heat gun on again and tackle another smooth surface.

If you can't get the hang of that, you should sit this dance out.

The resulting surface will be so smooth, in fact, that you need do little more than a light sanding before you restain it.

REPAIRING

Materials needed: wood filler

Tools needed: seam roller, putty knife, cloth

Age and misuse can do cruel things to any surface, but what it does to wood makes cellulite look like something you might actually want to have. Once the paint is removed, you could find deep pits or gouges in the wood's surface. It might bring back those horrible memories of how your skin would break out on the day before your junior prom. Yech, gross! Wood filler is furniture's version of Clearasil and can be applied to even out the surface very easily. It comes in a large variety of colors to match any wood and should be blended in gently with a putty knife and then smoothed in until the surface is even.

Another form of repair that you can easily do is fixing the veneer. If you have *loose veneer*, you need to take a small putty or palette knife and gently lift the veneer from the surface. Take a small brush and try to clean out anything that might be trapped beneath it. You can get at the old glue by dipping a Q-Tip in solvent or hot vinegar and swabbing it in the spot.

You now want to reapply glue under the surface. A Q-Tip dipped in glue makes a good applicator here, too. Finally, cover the area you are fixing with a small piece of waxed paper and then clamp it into place until the glue has dried. If, after it is dry, you find any excess glue that has oozed out of the space, remove it with a chisel or knife.

For **blistered veneer** you will have to slice into the wood grain with a small craft knife, then lift as you did above to clean out any debris. Put a thin piece of wood underneath the crack to lift it up, hold it there, and then squirt carpenter's glue into the blister. Roll the blister closed with a seam roller, then place on top the waxed paper and clamp we described earlier. If any glue appears underneath the seam of the blister when it is dry, hold a ruler with a metal edge against it and slice away the excess with a craft knife.

Incidentally, if sections of your veneer are actually missing, you will need to have it professionally repaired since, in all likelihood, you will have to replace the entire veneer.

Tip #5: As Handy As the Kitchen Sink

Believe it or not, there are a few items right in your cupboard that can be handy when it comes to furniture repair.

1. If the veneer isn't too badly lifted or loose, cover the area with a damp towel and press down on it with a warm iron. The heat from the iron might be enough to make the glue restick.
2. Instead of using a seam roller to smooth out the blister in your veneer, a rolling pin will work just as well.

FINISHING

In this case, "finishing" doesn't mean you are "finished." Your wood is now naked and must be dressed before you can present it to company. The forms of the *finishing* can vary but, whether you decide to repaint your furniture or restain it, don't even think of touching it until the wood has dried out thoroughly from the stripping. Leaving it overnight will do it in most cases, but if you live in a particularly humid area or if you are doing your work in the basement, that might not be enough time to do the trick. *Be patient!* This is very important. Remember that wood is porous and paint and stain can seep in unevenly, so if your wood is too wet, you are really asking for trouble. In other words, do not restain your chairs on the day before your new boss is coming to dinner—that is, not unless you think she'll find it amusing that her new pink Chanel suit has a mahogany stain right where the sun don't shine.

Painting

Materials needed: paint, brush

Paint is the easiest finish to apply to your old furniture and can be used if you are going for a country look or if the grain of the original wood wasn't so hot to begin with. You will probably need two coats, depending on the degree of coverage you want, and you should follow the same instructions we gave for painting woodwork in chapter 5.

By the way, painted furniture has become very popular of late. At many high-end antique stores we have seen armoires and cabinets that are painted a grass green or a mixture of yellow and pink. Often little flowers or borders have been painted on, too. So, if you are really creative, you can whip up some really unique furniture for yourself. (More about that, later in this chapter.)

CHOOSING YOUR PAINT

Here, as in the previous chapter on painting, you have two paint choices: *water* or *oil based*.

While **water-based paint** is certainly easier to use and has a quicker cleanup time, it can raise the wood grain, scratch more easily, soften if you live in a moist climate, and only be applied in thin coats. For these reasons, it is best used on **children's furniture**, on **cabinets**, and on **woodwork**.

Oil-based paint has a more scratch-resistant finish, is less affected by moisture, does not raise the grain, and dries to a smooth finish. It is, however, more toxic and slow-drying. It is best used on **stairs** and **railings, floors** and **doors, woodwork**, and **previously finished wood**.

APPLYING YOUR PAINT

In general, painting wood is no different from painting walls. The preparation of the wood surface is the key, so make sure that you have completed your sanding and stripping phases very carefully. If you are working with previously painted wood, check that all chips and dents in the surface have been repaired, then prime. Wood with a clear finish should have the previous top coat stripped and then it should be primed in order for the paint to stick.

When **priming** use a water-based primer if you are going to be using a water-based paint and an oil-based primer for an oil-based paint. Check to make sure you are not leaving brush marks behind. If you see one, sand over it with 220-grit sandpaper when the primer is dry.

Mask any area of your piece that you do not want painted or intend to paint in another color.

Apply a thin coat of paint, brushing in the direction of the grain. Hold the brush at a forty-five-degree angle from the surface and keep your application pressure light. After the first coat has dried, sand with 400-grit sandpaper and wipe off. Apply another heavier coat. If this is your last coat, do not sand, just wipe down. If you are going to be applying additional coats, sand and wipe each subsequent coat. Leave the last coat unsanded.

Tip #6: Bring On the Heavy Artillery

If you are painting furniture that is going to be put in a child's room or in another area of heavy use, you will want to apply a clear coat of polyurethane when you are done. If you used oil-based paint, use an oil-based polyurethane and a water-based one over latex.

Wet-sand the painted surface with slightly moistened 600-grit wet/dry sandpaper and then wipe down before applying the top coat.

Antique-ing

Have you noticed how the noun *antique* has taken on new life as a verb? "Antique-ing" is *the* baby boomer Sunday sport, surpassing "croissant-ing" and "New York Times-ing" in most large, urban areas. It must give antiques dealers a good chuckle to see the BMW set traipsing out to their stores to fight over stuff *they* dug out of some musty old garage. Joan has a friend who has gotten so hooked on the flea market craze that he will fly halfway across the country for a good chance to antique. While his home is beautiful, it is a bit disconcerting to enter a room that is completely filled with portraits of other people's dead relatives.

Well, you can make your own "antiques" by buying either an inexpensive piece of old furniture to refinish or by getting something at one of the unfinished or naked furniture stores and mimicking the kind of paint jobs you see in the higher-end stores. Look around and don't be afraid to steal from the designers. What, Martha Stewart is coming to dinner next Saturday? So, who's gonna know? No one, except us—and we promise not to tell.

The most popular form of antique-looking paint is the worn-out, farmhouse look made popular in poor rural areas. Remember the kind of house your mother used to "tsk, tsk" over? Well, now you too can have furniture that looks as if it's been used and used and used. Fashions are strange, aren't they?

Country-style distressing is very easy to do:

1. Apply a thin coat of a wood stain and then cover it over with shellac.
2. When it has dried, put a layer of water-based paint on top and let it dry, too.
3. With a piece of 100-grit sandpaper, sand off selected areas of the surface. Sand some parts with a heavier hand than others so it has the uneven look of time taking its toll. Sand the corners, too, as well as any area that has a raised-up detail.
4. Wipe down the piece to remove all particles left by sanding.
5. Apply denatured alcohol and, *voilà*, your house, too, will look like a barn. . . . This is a good thing?

Stenciled Designs

For those of you who flunked Art 101, stenciling is an especially fun way of doing up a child's room or a kitchen. You can buy stencils of cars, planes, trucks, flowers, etc., at any craft store or you can make your own. Tape the stencil down to a dry wood surface and then fill in the center with an acrylic paint by dabbling it onto the center surface of the stencil. Use a stencil brush and work until the entire area is filled in. Wait until the paint is dry before you remove the stencil.

If you are using more than one color, apply them one at a time and let each color dry before moving on to the next.

Color Washes

If you are painting on a piece of bare wood and all you want is a transparent coat of color, **color washing** is the best method to use. Add four parts of water to one part of water-based paint before you use it. Move the paint following along in the direction of the grain. You can use either a brush or a cloth to apply but, if you use a brush, wipe down as soon as you apply to keep the color light and see-through. If you want it to be darker, do it again. If it gets too dark, scuff it up when it is dry.

Staining

Materials needed: stain, paintbrushes, cloth, fine sandpaper

Staining is tricky since the combination of a spreading stain with porous wood can make for results that are a little unpredictable. Relax, though, because even the pros have trouble with this one. If you already like the color of the wood you find when you uncover it, applying a clear stain will preserve it for you while, at the same time, refreshing the surface. If you want the wood to be lighter, try bleaching it before you apply the clear stain. If you want something darker or different in tone, however, you're gonna have to go for the heavier stuff.

There are a few different types of stains you can use: *oil, water*, and *alcohol stains*.

OIL STAINS

Oil stains are generally the easiest to apply and work best with soft woods like pine or those with more open grains like mahogany. Be warned, however, oil stains are the most expensive, don't mix with other top coats, dry slowly, and are a mess to clean up.

1. Before you apply the stain, prepare the wood by applying shellac that you have thinned out with alcohol (probably one part shellac to four parts denatured alcohol). This will help ensure that the stain doesn't darken the wood unevenly by seeping into the grain of the cut end of the wood.
2. Let the shellac dry for about three hours.
3. Use either a brush or a cloth to apply the stain. Apply with even strokes, going along the direction of the grain.
4. Wait another fifteen minutes before taking a clean cloth and wiping off the excess stain.
5. If it looks okay, let sit for twenty-four hours before sealing.

WATER STAINS

Water stains are really more of a dye than a stain and are considerably less expensive than the oil variety. You've got a certain amount of preparation to do here as water stains start out life as powders to which you add boiling water.

Before you apply them, you have to make sure that the grain of the wood is raised to a sufficient level that it can take the stain evenly. You do this by using a sponge dipped in warm water on the whole surface, then letting the wood dry for three more hours. Sand it well with number 220 paper, and you're ready.

The water stain can be applied with a spray gun for ease, but a brush or cloth works well too. If you decide to go with the second method, work fast since the stain soaks in almost as fast as you apply it.

ALCOHOL STAINS

Alcohol stains are kind of a hybrid stain. While they leave a very sharp color like the oils, they don't wear as well as the water stains. Before applying the stain, you will need to coat the surface with a high-gloss varnish to which you have added an equal amount of turpentine. Here, too, you can use a spray gun, brush, or cloth and you must work fast. Errors are harder to control with this type of stain, but you can put another coat on top, if you want.

Tip #7: To Err Is Human

As we mentioned above, wood is a difficult surface to control and, therefore, errors frequently occur during the staining process. Of these, **blotching** is the one that happens most often. In order to figure out if your wood might blotch, try a small amount of your stain on a hidden area of the wood. If it blotches, you will want to use a preventive measure before moving on to the whole surface.

One way to prevent the blotching is first to fill in the small holes or pores that appear in the wood with a **stain controller**. You apply the controller with a brush or rag and use enough so that it is totally absorbed into the wood. Once the wood is saturated with the controller, you should apply the stain at once. If you wait too long, the controller will have dried up and its benefits will have been lost.

GEL STAINS

Gel stains are a good idea since you don't just pour them on as you do the others, and thus you can control their degree of penetration better. They are thick and similar to wall paint in texture and will move around the wood only if you push them along with your brush. Gels are great for woods like pine and cherry which cry out for even staining, but some other woods that need a much deeper penetration to bring out the depth of the grain will not fair as well.

Tip #8: I See Spots Before My Eyes

If, by some horrible chance, the stain dries in spots before you can wipe off the extra, you may be stuck. If you catch the spots before they are totally dry, however, you can reverse the process by either applying more stain to even it out or by adding thinner to the stain before it sets so it will soften up enough to be just wiped off.

If you're too late, you might have to restrip, resand, and restain the area; and if you're not superspeedy this time, history will repeat itself. Usually we just say Haste Makes Waste, but in this case, If You Snooze, You Lose.

SEALING

Materials needed: oil, brushes, cloth, fine sandpaper, shellac, alcohol

After you've gotten your furniture all spruced up with a new coat of paint or stain, you want to make sure it stays that way. In order to do that, you'll need to apply a *finishing coat*. The finish can come in the form of an *oil* or a *lacquer*.

Oils provide the most natural-looking finishes and are good for the wood, too, since they nourish it as they penetrate the grain. *Tung* and *orange oil* are natural while *Danish* and *teak oil* are synthetic resins. Both kinds are applied to a dry surface with a cloth. It's a good idea to rub the oils in well—think of it as giving your armoire or dining room table a massage. Let the oils sink in for about half an hour, then wipe off the excess.

The next day, if you want, you can repeat the process and, if the surface is used a lot, apply a third coat on the day after that. To make it really shine, after the final coat has dried, buff it with very fine steel wool which you have dipped in the oil and then wipe the whole surface dry.

If you like a *much* shinier surface, you'll have to use a *varnish* or *shellac*. This is best for painted surfaces as well as coarser-grained woods. You can either mix your own varnish by adding denatured alcohol to the shellac or you can buy a ready-made kind like a polyurethane gloss that is especially quick drying. If you use the latter, apply the coats very thinly, working in the direction of the wood grain. Work rapidly and try to keep the starting and stopping of the strokes invisible by beginning each new stroke in the middle of the previous one and then overlapping the edges, slightly. After the first coat has dried (probably two hours), and you have lightly sanded the piece and then removed all the extra dust, you can apply a second coat.

Tip #9: Psst . . .

Some of the newer lacquers come in spray cans. If you go this way, make sure you keep the sprayer moving backward and forward, making long sweeps. The spray should be applied close to the surface and you should overlap the applications as you go along.

Spray lacquer dries really fast, so you should only need to wait an hour between coats.

Tip #10: Age Before Beauty

If you want the stained piece to look "antiqued," skip the sanding part of the process and leave it rougher looking: a high and smooth gloss will ruin the effect.

PRESERVATION

Here's something we know you all can relate to: preserving the delicate surface of your furniture requires some maintenance. Yes, ladies, as with our skin, the elements and the environment surely do take their toll on our wooden goods.

Furniture preservatives come in the form of an *oil* or a *paste wax*. Both types of products nourish and protect your furniture.

Wax is often thought of as a top coat in its own right, but what it really does is beautify and protect the oil finish you applied under it. It can absorb tiny scratches and, when applied thickly, forms a hard shell to protect your furniture from the rigors of daily use.

The more layers you apply, the harder the finish. You want to choose a wax that has a very high ratio of wax to solvent and then really rub and buff it into the surface. This is another good way to get rid of frustration, and the results are beauteous.

Apply the wax with a cloth or a fine pad. After you apply it, allow it to dry for a few minutes and then gently wipe off the spots that remain. Now let it set again for about fifteen minutes before you start buffing. Use a circular motion on the wood to make sure that all traces of the wax are gone, then pick up the pace and continue until it is hard to the touch and shiny to the eye. Apply and buff another coat but, this time, let it dry for twenty-four hours before applying more. The next day apply two more coats in the same manner.

If there are detailed or carved areas in your wood, use a liquid wax and a stiff brush on them, then buff in the same manner as you did the flat areas.

Opinions vary as to how often you should wax your furniture. The minimum, for you lazybones, should be twice per year, for spring and fall cleanings, but we would recommend once a month, especially for your finer furniture.

TAKE FIVE

If you think all this work might just be a bit too much for a piece of secondhand furniture, we advise you to look at the humongous prices recently paid at celebrity auctions for virtually the same stuff. Who knows, if you become famous someday, your piece of refinished junk might just be peddled as a precious heirloom. However, if you do have an antique that you think may be valuable, or that you are interested in selling, check with a dealer before you refinish it. There are some pieces that are valued for their original finish, blemishes and all. Refinishing them can destroy much of their value.

10

Oh, Just Stick It In, Already!

SETTING UP AND WIRING YOUR VCR AND STEREO

In most households throughout this great land of ours, the tasks of setting up the VCR and stereo systems are usually left to the men. Actually, it's not so much a case of "left to" as it is a fact that men look upon their ability to tackle complex electronic equipment as their God-given birthright. In fact, not being able to put all those little wires and holes together is tantamount to a slight against their virility. Well, if we were to take all those flashing 00:00s on VCRs as a signpost of a man's potency, we'd have to say that no one had to worry about overpopulation in the future.

In fact, it has become so easy to create an ever-expanding entertainment universe for yourself that (dare we say it?) anyone can do it—and that includes men. In this chapter, we will take you on a guided tour of some of the basic parts that come with VCRs and stereo systems and teach you how to read those overly intricate instructions that accompany your purchases. We know that most of you have gotten so frustrated trying to follow the "connect A to C" type directions that you've probably wanted to just pound your little fists against the wall and cry. Uh, uh, uh . . . we'll have none of that, if you please. Just stick with us and we will take the misery out of entertainment.

THE VCR

Who'd ever have thought that this little device, designed for your pleasure, no less, would prove to be the source of so much difficulty. From the second you enter the appliance department at your local store, you are bombarded with a series of questions that appear to require a Ph.D. to respond to correctly:

1. Is your TV cable ready?
2. How many heads do you want?
3. How many hours programmable?
4. Remote?
5. Standard, long, or superlong play?
6. You do want VCR Plus, don't you?
7. Do you want your sound in stereo?

HELP!!!

It's enough to make you run from the store holding your head and screaming "Forget it . . . network movies with commercials are fine with me!" And just think, all this happens *before* you even unload the little sucker and see the wires and connecting cables that come with it.

In reality, those questions are really just meant to confuse you into buying the most expensive model. We'll just tick off the most likely answers for you:

1. Almost all TVs bought since the end of the Vietnam War are cable ready.
2. *You* only need one head, but your tape-recording habits will best determine if a two- or four-head system is best for you. Since there's really not that much difference in price, you might as well go for the four heads.
3. Again, the number of hours you want to be able to program is based on how much you plan to record. Although the capacity to program fourteen events over a period of seven days is nice, where the hell are you going to be that you won't be able to get back to your TV for over seven days and, besides, are there really fourteen events that are even *worth* programming? So, unless all you'll be thinking about over your week's vacation is the episodes of *All My Children* you're missing, you probably don't need the high-end product.
4. Remote is a nice feature unless you get your daily workout by popping up and down from your sofa to your VCR and back again.
5. It is a big saving on tapes to have the ability to record at different speeds. A standard two-hour tape stretches to six hours when used in the superlong-play mode.
6. VCR Plus is a good thing if you do a lot of recording directly from your standard TV. With this option, all you have to do is check your TV listing for the code number next to the show you want to tape and then enter it into your VCR. This eliminates the chance that your VCR clock might be off or that you punch in the wrong channel and end up with the adult channel's premiere presentation of *Debbie Does Dallas* instead of The McLaughlin Group.

7. We don't know about you, but to us, the idea of having the sound of Jean Claude Van Damme laying waste to some scummy villain surround us or listening to Sylvester Stallone's car plowing into an extra-heavy-duty rig at seventy miles per hour coming at us from every corner of the room is not our idea of a relaxing evening at home. Men love having a stereo hookup for their VCRs. That way, when they watch the Super Bowl, they can pretend that they're really there. Well, to that we say, "bah, humbug." Give us Wynton Marsalis in stereo . . . give us the Beatles' reunion in stereo . . . even give us Smashing Pumpkins in stereo, but let us watch TV without feeling as if a train wreck is occurring in our own living rooms.

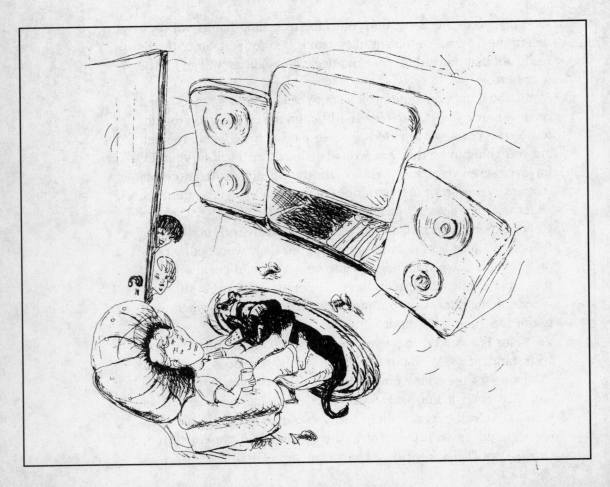

Your Mission, Should You Choose to Accept It . . .
The Setup

Once you've finally made your choice and you bring the VCR home, pour yourself a nice glass of Chardonnay and settle down for an evening of the grown-up's version of connect the dots. In reality, most of the instructions only look hard. They are actually relatively easy to follow.

Most hookups are predicated on whether or not you have either an **antenna/cable** connection or you are using a **monitor/receiver**.

ANTENNA/CABLE CONNECTION

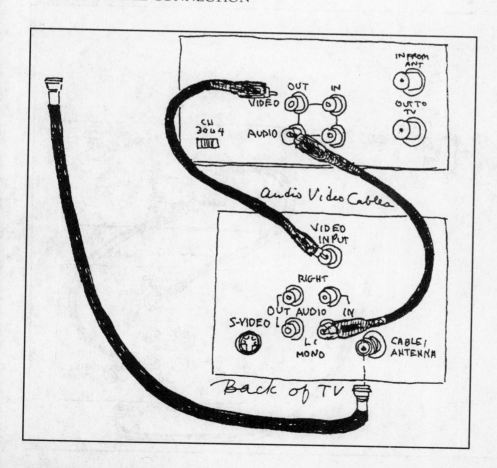

Oh, Just Stick It In, Already!

If you are using an outside antenna or an antenna that is attached to your TV physically, via either rabbit ears or a bow tie setup, all you have to do is set the channel switch on the back of your VCR to the correct channel indicated (usually 3 or 4) and then connect the leads from the antenna to the VCR and, finally, connect the VCR to your set. After you plug in your power cords, you are ready to go.

If your TV is cable ready, i.e., you do not use a cable box to obtain your cable reception, you proceed in the same way.

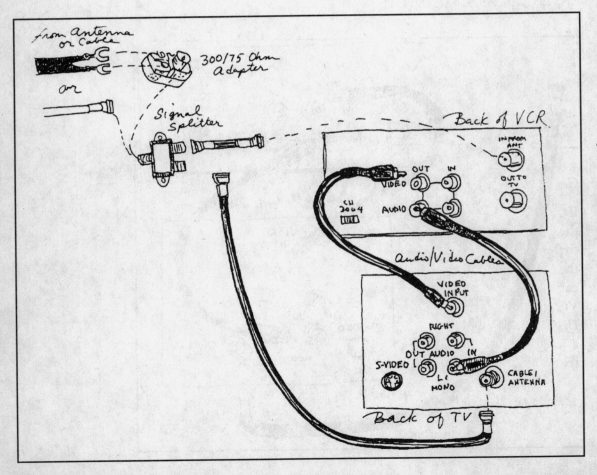

Tip #1: Splitting the Difference

You can improve the quality of the picture you receive when using this type of hookup if you use a **signal splitter** and two **audiovisual cables** to aid in your hookup.

1. Connect the signal splitter to the antenna or cable leads and then attach two **coaxial cables,** one to each little knob which you will see on the signal splitter. (One coaxial cable will come with the VCR, but you'll have to buy one extra.)
2. Take the other end of one of the coaxial cables and connect it to the cable or antenna knob at the back of the TV. Take the other cable and attach it to the **IN** knob at the back of the VCR.
3. The last thing you have to do is attach the two **audiovisual cables** (you will need to buy these separately). One of them will connect the **Video Out** knob on the back of the VCR with the **Video In** knob on the back of the TV. The second cable will connect the **Audio Out** knob on the VCR with the **Audio In** knob on the TV.

This system will allow you to switch back and forth from the TV to the VCR without having to hit a special button.

CABLE BOX CONNECTION

If your television gets its cable reception through the use of a box which the cable company supplied, connect the *cable wire* which comes from the wall to the *In* knob on the cable box. Then connect the *Out* knob on the cable box to the back of the *VCR's In Antenna* knob via a coaxial cable. A second coaxial cable will lead from the *Out To TV* knob on the *VCR* to either the *Cable/Antenna* knob on the *TV* or to the *VHF and UHF* knobs on the *TV*. If you use the latter method, you will need to buy a *75 to 75/300 Ohm separator* to connect to the second coaxial cable as the VHF and UHF connection has two knobs on it.

You can use the signal splitter method here, too, if you attach the *signal splitter* to the wall cable wire and then attach one knob of it to the *In* knob on the cable and the other to a second coaxial cable which will lead to the

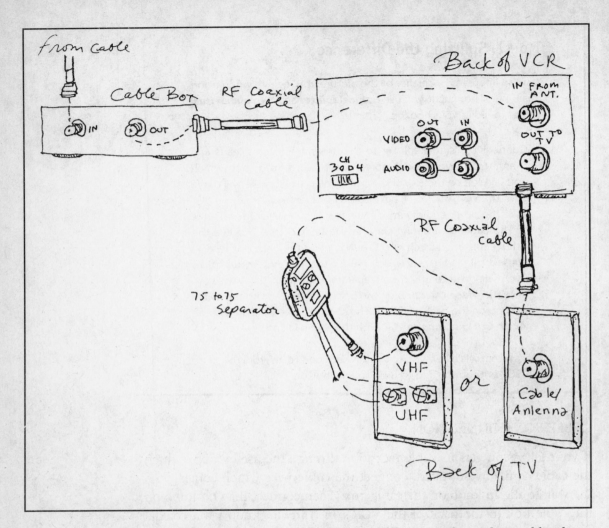

cable/antenna knob on the TV. You will do the Audio and Visual hookups in the same way as was described above using two **audio/visual cables**.

We hope that that was as much fun for you as it was for us because, trust us, we had a blast.

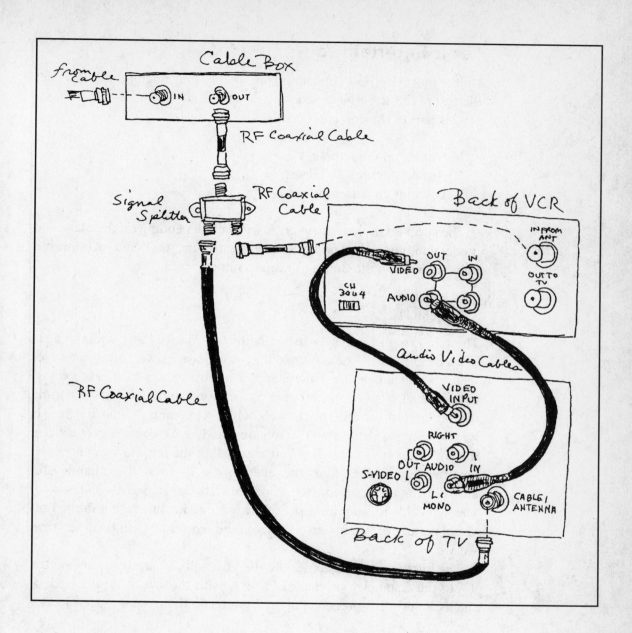

Let It Entertain You

Unlike most electrical appliances, just simply plugging in the VCR is not the end of the story. Now you have to set it up.

This part of the operation involves:

1. Setting up the remote
2. Setting the time and date
3. Learning how to program

The specifics of these three areas will vary depending on the make and model you buy, so it is best to follow the manufacturer's instructions, but there are a few basic things to keep in mind.

THE REMOTE

The remote will need at least **two batteries**. Always keep extras or a set of rechargers in the house since they don't last forever. Men can never seem to remember this. How many of us (by a show of hands, please) have walked in on our loved ones as they were in the middle of bashing the remote on the side of the sofa while screaming, "What the hell is wrong with this damn thing?" I'm sure you, like us, could barely conceal the smirk on your face when you asked, "But, honey, did you check the batteries?" and then took the offending item from their hands and changed the batteries yourself. Moments later, after peace was restored, were you able to keep from sticking your tongue out at them in the universal gesture of "I told you so"? If you did, you're all better women than we are.

The instructions that come with the VCR will usually say to tune in the TV to the channel you selected (3 or 4) with the switch on the back of the VCR and then press one of the buttons on the remote to activate it.

THE TIME AND DATE

When you first turn on the VCR, you will be greeted by the flashing 00:00 we mentioned earlier. Now, you can leave it like that under the rationale that you have enough other clocks in the house from which you can tell time, but no one will be fooled. Those flashing digits will be screaming to all your visitors "I can't program my VCR" and you will be looked upon with pity.

'Tis a far, far better thing to brave the twists and turns of the directions in your manual and hope for the best. Although they vary, they usually involve following a system of numbers that represent the day of the week until you find the one that corresponds to the correct day. Just press the indicated button on the remote to set it. Repeat the process for the hour and minute and then again to indicate if it is A.M. or P.M. If you've done it properly, you will be rewarded by having the correct time appear before your very eyes.

PROGRAMMING TO RECORD WHEN YOU'RE AWAY FROM HOME

This is the part that separates the men from the boys, so to speak. It's all well and good to use your VCR to watch tapes you rented from your local video store or to view home movies from your parents' fiftieth wedding anniversary, but that's all sissy stuff compared with being able to record a program straight from your TV.

VCR Plus makes it much easier since all you have to do is press the button on your remote which will display the main menu, go to the VCR Plus area, and then enter the **code number** printed beside the show you want to record in your newspaper's TV guide. Press **enter** on the remote and **turn off the VCR**. This part is very important since the act of turning it off will activate a timing device in your VCR that will kick in when the time for the coded show arrives. Leave your cable box turned on and tuned to the channel you want to record, however.

If you don't have VCR Plus, you'll have to rely on the more tried-and-true method that, in our opinion, is a little like playing Russian Roulette. Follow the directions in your manual and enter the day, date, and time of the program you want to record along with the channel it will appear on. We've heard of people who've had success doing this, but then, we've also heard of people who've seen the Loch Ness monster—so good luck.

It's Show Time

Your VCR can do two basic things: play prerecorded tapes or record from the TV. Above we showed you how to set your VCR to record when you are not there to press the buttons. If you are there, you can still use VCR Plus, or you can leave the TV on the usual number 3 or 4, put your cable box onto the channel you want to watch, press Record on your VCR, and it will do the rest. To watch a prerecorded tape, just put it in and press Play. It doesn't matter which channel your cable box is set to as it will be bypassed.

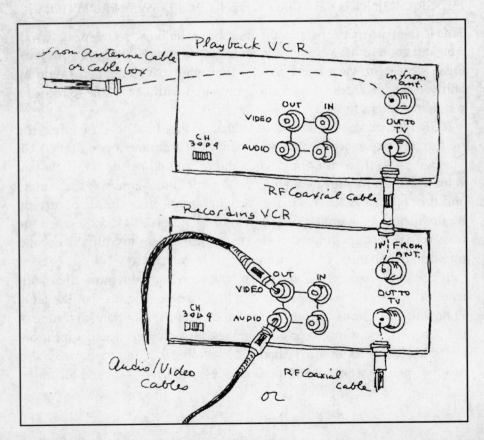

Tip #2: Hey . . . Wanna Buy a Hot Copy?

One other thing you can do with a VCR is make copies of other tapes. Now, we are not for one minute suggesting that you make copies of the tapes you rent—heavens, no—but we know that you'd just love to make sure that everyone in your family sees the cute tape you made of little Johnny taking his first steps. Obviously, you need another VCR in order to accomplish this but, once you have one, the setup is easy. Designate one machine as the player and the other as the recorder. Press play on the former and record on the latter and you are in business.

And One More Thing

Believe it or not, these machines were not meant to stand the test of time. About four or five years is all we've been able to get from an old fave before it has to be retired to that great VCR graveyard in the sky. You can help to prolong the life of your machine, however, if you keep it covered with a dust jacket, use a VCR head cleaner periodically for maintenance, and take it in to be professionally cleaned and serviced once a year.

STEREOS

Remember the joy you felt when you rushed home with your first Herman and the Hermits album? How you tenderly wiped it down and then put it on the turntable and, oh so gently, lowered the needle onto the first groove? Well, ladies, those days are as gone and forgotten as the hula hoop or, for that matter, Herman and the Hermits.

In place of the simple little hi-fi you just had to plug in, we now have amplifiers and receivers and speakers and hundreds of other components that are all supposed to add up to the stereo system of your dreams. First you have to wander through the store until you find parts that give you the correct balance of bass and treble you like. And what ensemble would be complete without a cassette deck and CD player? The size of the area in which you intend to put your "entertainment center" also must be considered as some of these units can take over an entire room. Of course, if you have no space but are on the higher end of the spending food chain, you can even attach some of the new European models directly to the wall where their wafer-thin shapes take up no more space than a small bookcase.

The problem with all this selection business is that, eventually, you will have to connect them in order to make them work. After all, appearances are one thing, but you bought the thing to listen to it, not just to admire it.

The first thing you have to determine before setup is where in the room you want your speakers. Then, you can work backwards from there. Position your speakers so that they surround the area where you will do your listening but are not right on top of you. Once you have got that set, choose the place where the cabinet for the components will be placed. It doesn't matter how close it is to the speakers. You will probably want to chuck those measly wires that came with the system since they are never long enough.

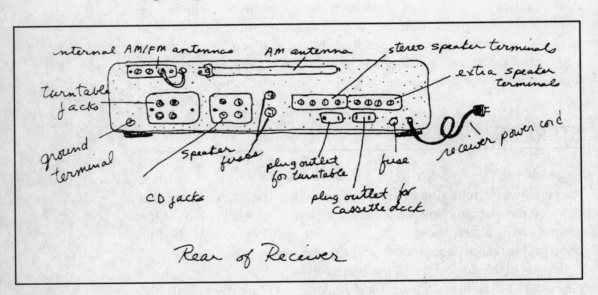

Your actual setup can vary according to design, but usually the receiver goes on the bottom with the CD and cassette decks on top of it and the turntable (if you have one) on top of that. All the separate parts are then connected to the receiver via a series of cables. The back of the receiver should be marked with several sets of *jacks*, each marked for their use (i.e., cassette deck jacks, CD jacks, etc.). The back will also have places that resemble electrical outlets where the cassette deck and turntable can be plugged in. The speakers are attached to their appropriate terminals on the deck of the receiver via wires that run from the base of the speakers. If you are going to replace the existing wires on your speakers with longer ones, you will need to cut them with wire cutters, strip the plastic covering off, and then repeat the process with the ends of the new wires. When the copper ends of both wires are exposed, you can splice them together. Make sure that the receiver is not plugged in until the process is complete.

By the way, it's not a good idea to plug in the receiver until after all the components have been attached.

TAKE FIVE

Now that your entertainment systems are complete, it's time to have a party. Hey listen, we'd have a party to celebrate the opening of a new Macy's, so why not for this?

As you're wining and dining your guests with some smooth sax music playing in the background, don't be surprised if, when you happen to glance over at either your VCR or your stereo system, you catch some man fiddling with it. Smile indulgently as his hands ruin the gentle sound balance you have so carefully achieved. Grit your teeth when he turns on the TV to whatever sporting event is playing on ESPN. It's in their genes; they just can't help themselves.

CHAPTER

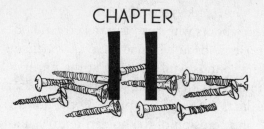

11

Is That a Wrench in Your Pocket, or Are You Just Glad to See Me?

HOW TO TALK TO REPAIR WORKERS, CONTRACTORS, AND OTHER SERVICEPEOPLE

Picture this: You are standing in three feet of dirty, soapy water as the level in your sink is steadily rising. Before you stands a man in overalls and heavy boots who has just tracked mud onto your freshly shampooed carpet. He holds in his hand a large wrench and your dog is making ugly growling sounds while looking at the fingers of his hand as if they were five, mustard-laden, ballpark franks. He is talking to you and using words like, "O-ring," "slipped to the fourth joint above the fracture level," and "erosion of the golden temple" (at least it sounds something like "golden temple"). Your eyes are glazing over and you imagine you are back in tenth-grade calculus listening to Miss Staniforth explain a complex theorem. Suddenly, you hear something that jolts you back to reality: "The total will come to four hundred and eleven dollars for parts and labor."

WHAT IS WRONG WITH THIS PICTURE?

Basically, you have just succumbed to the worst trap in home repair: you have allowed a repairperson to lead the band. Now, true, you called him because you have a problem, but you didn't do your homework and now you are standing there, ignorant not only of the correct questions to ask but also of the few simple terms that might give you a road map to his long and technical explanation. Trust us, you are a repairperson's dream and will probably be the brunt of a good story over a few brewskis that night. ("You should've seen her face when I told her her golden temple had eroded!" . . . see, you did hear it right.)

Now, this is not to suggest that all repairpeople are unscrupulous, because they aren't. Rather, having a little knowledge about what you want and learning to ask the right questions can save you the time, money, and embarrassment of getting swept away by a string of jargon and useless technical explanations. Let's face it: you don't need to know the history of pipe fitting in America to know that you need a washer to be replaced, but your ability to cut to the chase just might save you a few dollars, not to mention the time to do something else that is more important (like going to work, to the gym, or to the sale on Christian Dior undergarments at your local lingerie store).

So, we want to go over with you a few tips on the care and feeding of re-pair people and contractors. There are seven important points to remember:

1. Recognizing when you need help
2. Finding the proper helper
3. Familiarizing yourself with the problem
4. Getting it in writing
5. Supervising the job
6. Making sure you don't change your mind
7. Making nice

Recognizing When You Need Help

There are two types of help you will need: **voluntary** and **involuntary**. In order to distinguish between the two types, it might be useful to think of your house the way you think of your body.

Voluntary help is like plastic surgery—nice to have, but hardly life threatening. In other words, will eliminating those bags under your eyes affect your ultimate health or will it just make it easier to get a date? In the same way, adding onto your deck or remodeling the den are the home's equivalent of a face-lift or liposuction. Joan did have a plastic surgery emergency, however. While spending a Christmas week at a spa in Palm Springs, she decided to go for a walk. It was a lovely day, and so she decided to take a short cut through the hotel's garden. Imagine her surprise when the open door to the sunshine turned out to be an extra-clean window to pain and destruction. Yes, that's right—Joan walked smack bang into a plateglass window and broke her nose, leaving behind two little smudge marks showing the place where her nose and the glass met. Needless to say, she had to have her nose done, something she had been thinking about since the age of sixteen, but had never had the guts to try. She even got her insurance to foot the bill.

Most of us are not so lucky. The home equivalent to Joan's saga would be if a recent storm left a small water spot on your dining-room wall and you used the opportunity to get the whole room repainted a lovely shade of peach instead of the sickly green that came with the house when you bought it.

So, voluntary help in a house occurs when you have the time and energy to research exactly what you want done and who would be the best person to do it.

Involuntary help is more like waking up with a stabbing pain in your right arm—you better get it looked at fast! Exploding pipes, winds that knocked trees through your living-room window, earthquakes, and floods are situations calling for immediate action. Involuntary help also includes the times when you have a problem that you have tried to solve on your own but have finally decided is way beyond your meager skills to fix. We've outlined some of those situations earlier: badly overflowing toilets, major trouble with appliances, problems with your circuit breakers, etc. In all those situations, you are going to have to call in a professional.

Finding the Proper Help

Again, whether or not the situation is voluntary or involuntary will help determine your procedure here, too. For emergencies, it would be useful to have done your research earlier, in the same way you would for a voluntary situation. *Before* you need them, find out the names of the best plumber, electrician, etc. Also, having a good, all-purpose handyman in your Rolodex isn't a bad idea.

One of the best ways to assemble your list of little helper elves is to ask around among your friends and neighbors. But, as the old adage goes, "Consider the source." It probably isn't the best way to go to inquire about a plumber from the woman down the block who seems to have a plumber's truck permanently parked in front of her house. If he has to come back that often, he obviously isn't doing it right the first time (unless, of course, it isn't her sink pipes he's cleaning during those afternoon tête à têtê's).

Make sure you check the contractor's license and references. On a big job, don't just call the references, take the time to go look at a job or two. One person's idea of "good" may not be yours. In addition to asking if they were satisfied with the work, ask your sources what, if any, additional costs were realized and if the workers adhered relatively closely to an established timetable. Bear in mind that there are almost always some delays and cost overruns; the question is how much and why. Was the contractor unreliable or did the client change her mind five times? If you find someone you really like but you get a negative referral on him, check another reference, just to be safe. Just as there are unscrupulous contractors, there are also customers with unrealistic expectations.

Other good questions to ask are whether or not he has workman's compensation and, if he is using subcontractors or workers, whether he carries insurance for them. This is also the time to check your homeowner's policy, to make sure you are covered for accidents occurring in your home involving outside workers. The last thing you want is to find yourself supporting your nice painter and his family of five when he slips and falls off his ladder in your living room.

Familiarizing Yourself with the Problem

There are a few general rules of thumb to follow before you even start interviewing contractors. First of all—and we know this sounds obvious—figure out what you want done. For example, if it is just an electrical problem, that's easy enough, but if the work requires more than one discipline (e.g., in order to repair the broken pipe in your wall the wall needs to be torn out and then replastered and repainted afterwards), you might want to hire a general contractor who can supervise all the work that needs to be done. There are pros and cons to this method. The most obvious pro is that, once you have hired the general contractor, he takes care of hiring all the individual workers for each task, saving you the need to do so. The cons are that he will charge you for this little service and, if you are not careful, you could have no control over whom he hires. The way around the latter is to have him submit to you a selection of bids from the subcontractors so that you can evaluate which is the best way to go with your pocketbook in mind. This will save you from waking up to find that his brother-in-law and first cousin who just arrived in town from Cleveland have taken up formal residence at your construction site. As for the charge for his services . . . well, you don't get nuthin' for nuthin' in this world.

Next, try to learn as much as you can about what you need done. This will help you evaluate the information you will be given as well as allow you to ask better questions. Try to avoid using words like *doo-hickey* and *thingy* when describing parts and areas. Not only will you sound like an idiot, but it's a dead giveaway that you haven't a clue as to what you are doing. The person listening to you sees dollar signs when you mutter these inanities. Your local hardware or home repair store often has handouts that describe commonly used terms for all kinds of home repair items. If they don't, they might respond kindly to a damsel in distress. If you go that route, take notes that you can refer to later.

When your contractor is describing what he wants to do, one simple question will save you a lot of time and money: "Is that absolutely necessary?" Try to evaluate what needs to be done now, what you can wait to do later (providing it won't cost you more by waiting), and what is simply a nice extra you can live without. Men have known that secret for years when they go to buy a car, but the resulting toy sitting in your driveway shows that they don't practice what they preach. You can imagine that it's like going to the makeup counter—you definitely need something for washing your face, and having a good moisturizer is essential, but an eyelash-nourishing cream is probably just a luxury.

Don't Be Afraid to Say "No." As in any good relationship, you must set boundaries with your contractor. If he thinks he can push you into anything, you'll end up with paint made from the eggs of ancient Yaks found only in the Himalayas at $110 a gallon. Let him know what is important to you and what your budget is and make him stick to it. Trust us; he'll respect you more in the morning and, more important, so will you.

Get It in Writing

Think of this like a premarital agreement—do not enter into any work arrangement without a written agreement. Actually, Joan did let romance rule when she got married but, after getting a crash course in divorce, California style, that's not a mistake she'll make twice.

Have your proposed contractor submit a **written bid** that includes what he will do, what materials he will use, and the costs for his time, labor, and materials. The last thing you want is to be surprised with little extras. Establish when the clock actually starts ticking for him. For example, does it start when he leaves his house to get to you or when he arrives at your door? The condo Joan lives in recently hired a handyman to put up simple signs around the garage to indicate that it was a tow-away zone. Imagine their surprise when he submitted a bill for $350. The breakdown indicated that he charged for travel time from his house, which was about fifty miles away. Your contractor's commute is not your problem, nor is his choice to make his trek during the height of rush hour. If he's going to charge you for travel time, find someone who lives nearby.

If you are doing a big job and there is no hurry ("isn't that a contradiction in terms?" says Jeni, looking horrified), try to **get several bids** and then horse-trade them against one another to get the best price. Don't be afraid of a little haggling. It's a time-honored skill and could save you a tidy sum. But, one word of warning: The cheapest bid is not necessarily the best. That saving of money will, almost always, come as a trade-off for something else—quality of workmanship, materials, time taken to do the job, etc. Depending on your finances, the least expensive bid may be the way to go but, trust us, the difference between the lowest bid and the mid-range bid is almost always the price YOU will pay, one way or another.

Make sure that the terms regarding the **payment schedule** are also in writing. A good way to do this is to pay in three installments: Give one-third upon contracting for his services, another on commencement of work, and the rest after completion. If the work being done requires an inspection, make sure that you don't hand over the third sum until the inspection has been completed and okayed. If you are the one doing the inspection, that is just as valid. They don't get the dough until you are a happy camper. If the job is not only cosmetic but also involves tasks like plumbing, roofing, or wiring, you may want to hold back 10 percent of the fee for two weeks while you make sure everything works. In the excitement of finally finishing a major job and the relief of reaching an end of the chaos a repair situation can bring, it's easy to overlook a potential problem during the inspection. This is not an excuse to avoid paying the piper, but it will allow you time to check everything. An extra little dividend is that it will provide incentive to the tradesmen to come back if there's a problem. If he doesn't fix it, he doesn't get the rest of his money. Clever, huh?

Supervising the Experience

Once their work begins, so does yours. Remember that old Sunday School expression "Idle hands are the devil's playground"? Well, keep that in mind at all times. Jeni experienced a horror story when she, briefly, moved into a rented house following her divorce. The owner agreed to pay for some much-needed repairs and hired for the job a charming fellow named Tom whom they loved after his initial interview. Unfortunately, Tom was all foreplay with no follow-through, if you get our drift. When he *decided* to show up, he took more bathroom and rest breaks than a kindergarten student and knocked off early each day for an "emergency." Once, Jeni returned home to find Tom taking his break in front of her TV while catching up on the daytime soaps. He seemed so engrossed that she didn't want to interrupt him. It was only after he left that she saw he had made a feast of her leftover pot roast and Dutch apple pie and washed it all down with a bottle of Beaujolais Nouveau which Joan had brought home from a romantic rendezvous in Paris. Finally, Jeni decided she had had enough. Now when she has workers in the house, she makes sure that she is nearby to keep an eye on them.

This does not mean that you need to make a pest of yourself, but **do make your presence known**. Also, it is good to be available if something comes up that was not expected. Make sure that no expenditures beyond what you originally contracted for are added on without your approval. Now, obviously, if they hit a main water pipe and your house is in danger of floating away if they don't do something about it and you are sitting in the middle of a mud bath at the local spa, there should be room for some discretion but, short of that, make sure that there is somewhere to contact you.

Making Sure You Don't Change Your Mind

Now, we know that it's supposed to be a woman's prerogative, but whimsy costs—so think long and hard about any big job *before* you undertake it. Once a contractor has started a job it is often difficult, time-consuming (are you seeing dollar signs, yet? Well, here they come), and yes, *expensive* to make changes. Once you have decided where you want lights, what kind of finishes you want, and where your sink is to be placed, stick to it. Now, of course, there are occasions when you will discover that you have made a huge mistake (like the sofa you ordered won't fit in the place under where the lights will be hung), so if you think you have a doozy on your hands, don't wait. Call the contractor and *calmly* tell him or her your concerns. Shrieking "Oh, my God . . . oh, my God" is appropriate in the case of floods and pestilence but doesn't quite cut it here. Things may not be as bad as you think, and there probably is a solution that doesn't involve dynamite!

Is That a Wrench in Your Pocket, or Are You Just Glad to See Me? **255**

Make Nice

One other thing can make the repair and remodeling experience a better one for both you and your contractor—*make it a friendly relationship*. We don't mean you have to rush to him with plates of cookies or wear a fancy negligee, but offering an iced tea on a hot day or saying a few nice words can go a long way. As Joan's old grandmother used to say, "You can catch more flies with honey." We know it sounds simplistic, but it does make a difference. It can also help take some of the tension out of the experience for you, too.

AT THE STORE

Now we would like to explore how to get help and information at the local hardware store. A lot of women are intimidated when they enter these usually all-male domains.

First of all, don't look meek, embarrassed, or out of place. Try a little role-playing. Before you leave the house, go to the mirror, look yourself squarely in the eye, and say "hammerhead nails." That will get you in the mood. Now, you go, girl.

Once you're in the store, go to the section you need and **get the lay of the land**. You might just be able to figure out what you need on your own but, if not, at least the salesman will know you have a vague idea of what you are looking for. This is when it is a good idea to have either the piece you want to replace or a drawing of it with you. If you don't know what you will need, try to describe the situation you are trying to remedy in detail. Here, too, try to avoid using "girly" words to describe what you want. And if you are going to ask for help, look for the cutest salesman. We know, it's probably not politically correct to say stuff like that, but let's face it, there are distinct advantages to being a woman, and our motto is Use What You Got, and If You've Got It, Flaunt It!

Get a Load of That Woody!

BUILDING YOUR OWN (PROJECTS YOU CAN REALLY DO)

This chapter is kind of like the SATs of home repair; you've studied the basics, you've made a few simple applications, and now you're ready to see how they all work together. We have put together instructions for three types of projects that are, we think, relatively easy, useful, and fun. Not only that, they will impress the hell out of your friends when you proudly announce, "I did that." As you can tell, we have never been big believers in modesty.

To that end, we will teach you how to:

Build a freestanding bookcase,
Design and build an organized closet,
    and
Install track lighting.

We should warn you here: This is serious stuff, so don't expect our usual yucks along with the instructions. Well, we did digress a bit since we just couldn't help ourselves, but mostly we want your *undivided attention.*

BUILDING A BOOKCASE

In the chapter on drills, we showed you how to make bookshelves that are directly attached to the wall. Sometimes, however, you'll want a bookcase that can hold more weight or you want the luxury of being able to move a bookcase to a different room, if the whim strikes you; or you might live in an apartment that doesn't allow you to do any drilling in a wall. In those cases, you'll need a freestanding bookcase and, once you decide the shape and size you want, you're on your way.

Preparation

First establish *where* in your room the bookcase will go and *how much* you expect it to be able to hold. Next, *select your materials*. Of the many different types of wood, *pine* or *3/4-inch birch* or *oak plywood* (both sides veneered) are probably your best choices. You can also use *melamine*, which can be bought in 1x12, finished and predrilled, if you like.

Next, decide whether the shelves will have a *face frame* or be left as is. A face frame is a thin piece of wood nailed flat against the edge of the unit either to cover up the unfinished edge of plywood or for a decorative effect. Any solid lumber will be fine without a face frame, but if you use a plywood, you must finish the shelves with a face frame.

The bookshelf consists of **top and bottom shelves**, any number of shelves you want in between, and the **sides** and the **back**. The overall dimensions of the unit will be determined by how many shelves you want and the amount of space you will need between them.

Once you know how tall and wide the shelves will be, create a *"cut" list*. This is simply a list of all the pieces of wood or material you need with their appropriate dimensions. You can take this to a lumberyard and have them cut the wood for you, or use it as your guide and do it yourself. For the **back** of the bookcase, use wood with a thickness of 1/8 or 1/4 inch. It is probably best to have this piece cut at the lumberyard since this is the piece that will square the bookcase and, if it's even a little off, it won't work as well and your bookcase might be a bit tippy.

The very **top** piece will cover the entire width of the unit and will sit on the two side pieces. The **bottom** piece as well as the **intermediate shelves** will be the overall width minus the thickness of the two side pieces (since these pieces will sit inside the side pieces). It's better if the bottom shelf does not sit directly on the floor and you can get a base molding of, depending on your own aesthetics, between 1 1/2 to 3 1/2 inches to do the trick. When you go to figure the overall dimensions, keep in mind that the bottom shelf will be raised up by the amount you have chosen. If, say, you plan on storing records on the bottom shelf and you've left 1 1/2 inches between it and the floor, you will need to measure the position of the next shelf from the top of the bottom shelf, not the floor.

For the purposes of this example, we are going to use pine that is *1x12*. By the way, when we refer to lumber as 1 by 12, it is really 3/4 inch by 12 inches. The width of a piece of wood is always exactly as specified but, for some curious reason, the thickness is less. For example, 2 by is really 1 1/2, 4 by is 3 1/2 inches, and so on. This is probably some insider male-oriented code, but now you can be in on it, too.

The bookcase we will construct will have the following dimensions:

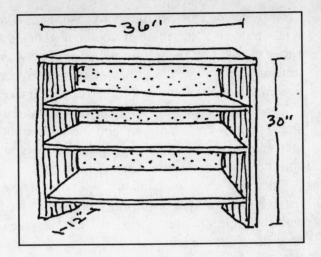

30 inches high
36 inches wide
12 inches deep.

In this case the **two side** pieces are each **3/4 of an inch wide**, so the bottom shelf is **1 1/2 inches** *shorter* than the top piece. The side piece will be the overall height, *minus* the thickness of the top piece, which is 3/4 inch. The back should be cut **1/8 inch** smaller on every side or **1/4 inch** smaller *overall*.

The following is a **cut list** for this bookcase.

CUT LIST

Top: *1 x 12 x 36*
Back: *1/8 x 35 3/4 x 29 3/4*
Bottom: *1 x 12 x 34 1/2*
Sides: *1 x 12 x 29 1/4 and all shelves*

Putting It All Together

You can either *nail* and *glue* or *screw* and *glue* the case together. If you use screws, buy a special drill bit for **countersinking**. These are sized to match the screws precisely, so double-check that they match.

1. Lay out all the pieces on a hard floor, finished edges down.
2. Mark on the sides where all the shelves will go.

3. If you are making adjustable shelves, drill the holes. The easiest way is to drill a line of holes that are 3/8 inch deep and insert small pegs specially designed for this purpose. (A 1/4-inch drill bit is the standard size for this.)

Tip #1:Sink That Bit

To drill a hole of a particular depth, wrap a piece of masking tape around the bit, clearly marking the desired length. When the drill has sunk in to the edge of the tape, the hole will be the right size.

NOTE: It is very important that all the holes line up on both sides of the bookcase, or the shelves will be crooked. You can make a template by predrilling a strip of wood, then marking the sides through the holes so that both sides will be exactly the same.

4. Attach the top to the sides.
   Lay one side and the top on the edge and run a bead of glue on the top edge of the side. Nail or screw the top to the side, then repeat with the other side.
5. Place bottom shelf against the marks on the sides, run a bead of glue on the ends and nail or screw it from the outside of the sides.

If the rest of the shelves are fixed, attach them in the same way. If they are adjustable, put the supports in the predrilled holes and slide the shelves into place. If you are making a tall bookcase with adjustable shelves, it's a good idea to make one shelf in the middle "fixed."

At this point the bookcase may feel unstable. Attaching the back will help square and strengthen it. If you have built it facedown, it's a simple matter of attaching the back as is. If not, turn the case over and proceed. Run a thin bead of glue and place the back in position. Straighten the bookcase against the back so it is square. Nail it into place with *small finishing nails*. You should nail it to the top, bottom, and sides. If the other shelves are fixed, nail it to them also. Turn the case over and make sure no glue has squished through. If it has, wipe it up with a wet sponge, otherwise it will show through when the wood is stained.

To finish it, glue and nail the base face in place with finish nails. This plate should run from the floor to the top edge of the bottom shelf.

Tip #2: Larger Can Be Better

If you want to make a larger bookcase with a **center support**, make the top and bottom shelves as above but cut the other shelves so that they are all attached to the middle support. Nail or screw the shelves on one half from the other side, then **"toenail"** the others in from underneath each shelf. Toenailing is simply nailing at an angle. This is done when you cannot nail straight on, as in a corner, or in this case, you are coming from underneath the shelf and going into the upright support.

Another option is to extend the base around both sides or to use decorative molding as faceplates.

Tip #3: A Whole Lot of Shakin' Goin' On

Even if you don't live in Southern California or another earthquake-prone area, it is a good idea to anchor all bookshelves directly to the walls.

Finishing

Since you have probably used unfinished or naked wood, you will need to finish the bookcase before you use it. Consult the chapter on wood finishing for your options and then follow those instructions for painting, staining, antiquing, and then sealing the wood.

REDESIGNING YOUR CLOSET

How many of you have ever stood in front of a jam-packed closet and wailed, "I don't have anything to wearrrrrrr"? If your hand isn't up, you're a dirty, rotten liar. Trust us, we've *all* done it. And what is the cause of our despair? A closet that is as topsy-turvy as your toy chest used to be when you were a kid.

Now, we're sure you've seen the insides of the closets they show on *Lifestyles of the Rich and Famous* and thought, "Oh, sure, it's easy for them to have neat, organized closets. They're rich and famous." Well, we're here to tell you that you don't have to be rich and it's certainly not necessary to be famous to have the closet of your dreams. All it takes is a little organization and some lumber and you, too, can have your blouses hanging in color-coordinated splendor and your shoes each resting in their own private little nest. It's an anal retentive's heaven and it can be yours, for the right price and a few nails.

Having a professional closet designer redo your closet can cost anywhere from several hundred to thousands and thousands of your hard-earned dollars. Here, we'll show you how to figure out how much space you need, show you some storage options, and give you a couple of sample plans that you can tailor to your own needs.

So . . . Do You Really Need Seventy-Five Pairs of Shoes?

In Jeni's case, the answer to that question is yes. They don't call her Imelda Munn for nothin'. Last year, she even got to smirk an "I told you so" when those platform shoes she'd been hoarding since the seventies came back into style. However, she freely admits that being a pack rat isn't necessarily a good thing. Sometimes even she must part with a beloved item or three. We guess that the moral of this story is: Before you spend your time redoing your closet, figure out if you really need everything that's in it.

As usual, we have a system to suggest how you go about doing this very thing. It is based on a principle we like to call the *"four piles and a*

trash can" theory of closet sorting: Sort all the contents of your closet into the four piles we describe below. If something doesn't fit the criteria of any of the piles, throw it the hell out!

PILE #1: The *"I'll wear it"* pile: stuff you use a lot and know you want to keep. (This pile should also include the sweater your Great Aunt Mary crocheted for you that she will be expecting to see you wear at the next Thanksgiving dinner party.)

PILE #2: The *"Goodwill"* pile: things that a still-usable tax deduction has moved you to donate to charity. This pile also includes what we all used to call "hand-me-downs" for friends and relations.

PILE #3: The *"I swear I'll repair it"* pile: holes, ripped hems, torn-off buttons—you know the drill. Before you put something in this pile, however, be honest with yourself—are you really the type to take thread to needle? Often our best intentions turn into years of procrastinating.

PILE #4: We like to call this the *"pile of last resort"*: Uh, huh, you all know what goes here—the things you haven't worn in five years and probably never will again but just can't quite bring yourself to get rid of. BEWARE OF THIS PILE! It is often a clothing scrapbook of failed romances and all those "special" days that meant so much to you way back when but now you can't really remember why. We don't care how good your old college boyfriend was in bed; it doesn't mean you still have to cart his letter sweater around with you for the rest of your life. Trust us: No one is that good!

Once you have separated all your things into their appropriate piles once, go through them and do it another time. The second time you must be brutal.

Now, here's where the trash can comes in. Do not let it leave your side for even one minute. As you go through your piles again, you will find that some items change from pile to pile and some won't find any pile to call home. These are the items that should go into the trash can. And if you are being honest with yourself, a lot of them will end up in the trash can.

Now for what we like to call the "Olympic moment." You have ten minutes to complete the following:

1. Take your "goodwill" pile, seal it up immediately, and, this is the important part, do not look inside it ever again! Run to your nearest drop-off point or arrange for it to be picked up while the force is still with you. (Putting the bags by the front door for three weeks just doesn't cut it. You'd be surprised how quickly three weeks can turn into forever.)

2. Move on to your repair pile. Here, you can take one last look, but remember, ladies, you have enough guilt in your life. Do not allow anything to remain that will be a reminder of what you haven't accomplished.

  Okay, you're heading down the home stretch . . .

3. Here the pace can slow for a minute for nostalgia time. Put on some soft music and wallow, briefly and for the last time, in the memories that your hot pants and thigh-high boots bring to mind. Don't weaken now—no pain, no gain. Uh-oh, we see we need to bring in the reinforcements: Close your eyes and conjure up the presence of . . . your mother. "Aren't you being selfish holding on to all these ratty old things with their golden memories? There are children in Africa starving for memories like these. So, share them a little bit, why don't you?" Good, we knew that would work . . . you're rallying . . . and . . . it's over!

If you've followed our system carefully, you should be left with only the stuff you're really likely to wear, a closet that has a whole lot more usable space, and the remembrance of why you left home in the first place.

Are Hemlines Up or Down This Year?

The first rule of good closet design is "A place for everything and everything in its place." Okay, Mom, you can leave us now. Well, in the end, Mother knew best. Life *is* simpler if you pick up as you go along, and that is easier to do if you have somewhere to put everything.

The best way to determine how much space you will need is to figure out how much space your wardrobe takes up. To help you do this, the following is a list of the common measurements of garments for men, women, and children.

WOMEN

Coats:	52 inches long	Handbags: Since ours are practically suitcases, who could tell, but usually, a shelf 3 inches wide by 12 inches deep will do it.
Dresses:	48 " "	
Skirts:	18–22 " "	
Blouses:	28 " "	
Jackets:	32–34 " "	
Shoes:	10 by 7 inches	Sweaters: 14 inches by 10 inches by thickness folded

MEN

Coats:	50 inches long	Shirts: 34 inches on hangers
Jackets:	38 " "	14 by 8 inches folded
Pants:	45 " "	Shoes: 12 by 9 inches

KIDS (This depends more than anything on how old they are, but these are average measurements for the wardrobe of a ten-year-old.)

Pants:	20 inches long	Shoes: 9 by 8 inches
Tops:	11 by 8 inches folded	Jackets: 24 inches long
Dresses:	25–30 inches	

With these measurements in mind, take a quick inventory of what clothes you actually have, multiply by the space they need, and you will be on your way.

Storage Options and Materials

Stores like Bed, Bath, and Beyond, Hold Everything, and closet design stores sell a huge variety of products that will make it easy for you to judge how you want your closet to look. You'll find a wide variety of options from shoe bags to tie racks to special drawers for jewelry. There are baskets that fit together or stack, sets of drawers on wheels, shelves, boxes, hanging bags for sweaters, and on and on and on.

Once you figure out what types of storage items you want, then you can decide what materials you want them in. Wire, melamine, and wood can be used either individually or in combinations for the shelves, drawers, etc., that will make up the component parts of your new closet. Take into account not only what you like but also what you can afford. In this case, the most expensive is not necessarily the best way to go. Melamine works just as well as wood, for example. Jot down the pieces you want and their measurements. When you get home, you can start designing by making scale drawings of how different combinations might look.

Some Design Basics

The major points to keep in mind when designing your closet are:

1. The amount of hanging space you will have
2. The types of doors
3. The shelving layout

1. In our opinion, the change that has had the most impact in closet design is the creation of a **double-hung section**. Since a traditional closet with only one rod leaves an inaccessible shelf above the rod and murky confusion on the floor, a double-hung-rod configuration will automatically double your useful space. We vote for trying to get as many things off the floor as possible.

When designing the layout of your closet, assume that the double hung rods will hang at about 82 inches and 42 inches from the floor, respectively. These measurements will accommodate most of the jackets, tops, and blouses in an average adult wardrobe, and the top rod will still be reachable.

A side note: Closets in older homes are about 28 inches deep, whereas newer homes are being built with closets of only about 22 inches in depth. Twenty-two inches is the absolute minimum that is still functional, but if you are building new closets from scratch, try to make them at least 28 inches deep. The extra room will allow you to hang shoe racks and other storage helpers on the door without squishing your clothes together.

2. When it comes to choosing what **type of door** you will have, there are various pros and cons to consider. Although sliding doors are attractive, they only allow you to see half of the closet at a time and they don't give you any space for hanging items on the inside. If, however, you don't have enough clearance for hinged doors to open into the bedroom, a sliding door may be your only option. Hinged doors, on the other hand, provide you with the opportunity to adapt them with shoe bags, racks, and other hanging holders but will cut into the overall depth of your closet. In general, we would always opt for hinged doors over the sliding variety, provided your closet is deep enough.

3. The decision as to what type of *shelving system* you want is very crucial, and your decision will be largely dictated by your available space. If you decide to use the wire shelving systems found in most do-it-your-self stores, remember that the brackets that support the shelves are 12 inches by 12 inches, therefore the shelves must be at least 12 inches apart.

One additional thought: Remember that clothes need air and shouldn't be crammed together. If you find you still don't have enough room, try to find other storage solutions, whether it be in other rooms, in storage bags under the bed, when not in season, etc.

Tip # 4: Taking You to the Cleaners

Many dry cleaners will store your cleaned garments for you on a seasonal basis. Frequently, this service is free or, at least, very reasonable. When we each lived in New York and in the kind of small apartments that New York is famous for, we discovered the secret world of dry cleaners' storage. Jeni, of course, could never quite figure out how the cleaner had the room to store everyone's clothes and had heard stories of people arriving to pick up their winter duds only to discover that they had mysteriously vanished. Since she never actually lost anything, however, she just put it down to one of those urban myths, like alligators in the sewer system. Still, before you send your clothes off to camp for the summer, it's probably a good idea to inquire as to what their replacement policy is—just in case your clothes fall into a black hole or are eaten by sharks.

A Sample Plan

To give you an idea of what we're talking about, we're going to start with a traditional 6-foot closet with two 30-inch, hinged doors and a single rod to be hung at 70 inches with one shelf above it. The wardrobe we will use to fill this closet consists of the following:

2 coats	6 belts
4 suits	12 dresses
6 pairs of pants	6 skirts
12 sweaters	15 blouses
4 pairs of jeans	10 tops
4 handbags—2 small, 2 large	2 dozen pairs of shoes

The dresses and coats can be hung together. Skirts can occupy single hangers along with the suits, or they can be hung on tiered hangers along with the dresses. Pants should be hung straight, rather than over a hanger and can double up with the dresses. Jeans and blouses can go on a double rod.

Since our sample closet has hinged doors that can be used for storage, we're going to put the shoes on the back of one of them and, on the other door, we will put a rack for belts and hooks for small handbags. We will fold sweaters and tops and place them either on shelves or in drawers or baskets.

By the calculations we gave you earlier, we will need:

30 inches of long hanging space
30 inches of double hanging space

The remaining 12 inches will be used for 12-inch-wide, wire baskets which have shelves on top.

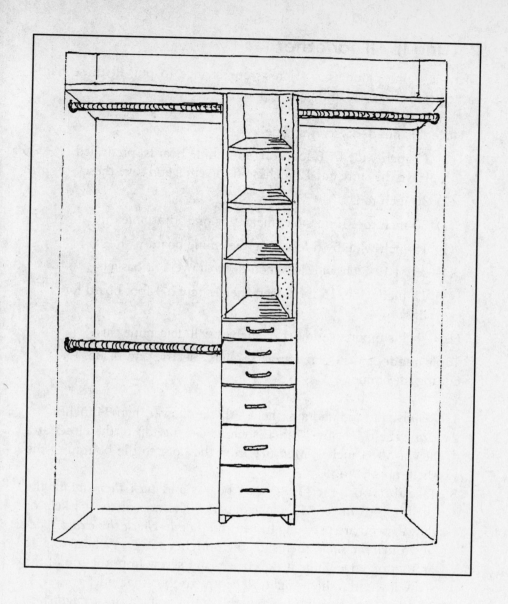

Putting It All Together

Okay, test time, kiddies . . . Here's your chance to put all those hard-earned skills to work and make a closet.

Materials needed: screws, glue

(2) 15-inch-wide by 8-foot-long melamine boards, predrilled. Have the store cut 12 inches off the ends and save these.

(2) 30-inch rods

(1) 30-inch rod. If possible, make this one adjustable.

(1) 15-inch-wide by 6-foot-long melamine board

(1) set of 12-inch-wide, 15-inch-deep drawers or baskets

(4) 12-inch wide, 15-inch deep shelves (cut a 4-foot board for this)

(16) shelf supports (number of shelves will determine this)

Tools needed: drill, screwdrivers, pliers, electric saw, blades for cutting melamine

1. *Remove* old rod and any shelves that are lower than 84 inches.
2. *Hang* the 6-foot-by-15-inch shelf across the top of the closet at a height of 84 inches. *Measure* from the floor to the bottom of the shelf, not the top.
3. Take the two 7-foot-by-15-inch boards and *tuck them under* the shelf approximately 12 inches apart. Take one of the baskets or drawers you are planning to use and *double-check the exact spacing. Mark the shelf*, then slide the uprights out. Run a bead of glue on the top edge, *slide* it into place, and *screw* from the top of the shelf down into the upright. *Repeat* with the other side.
4. The closet will probably feel unstable at this point, so to *strengthen it*, take one of the 12-inch-wide shelves and, just as you would in making a bookcase, *glue and screw* it at the bottom of the two uprights.
5. *Measure up* from the top of this shelf, and glue and screw another shelf right above where the drawers or baskets will be. Now your unit should feel stable.

6. **Attach** the top rods at 82 inches, and the lower one at 42 inches.
7. Following the manufacturer's directions, **hang** the drawers/baskets.
8. **Insert** the shelf hangers where desired and **slide** in the rest of the 12-inch shelves.
9. **Finish** off your closet by hanging the shoe rack over one door and the belt and handbag hooks on the other.

You may be so pleased with your new closet that you won't want to put anything back in it and instead just sit and admire it all day long. Since that wasn't exactly the object of all this hard work, put all your clothes away nicely and then go wild—do another one!

INSTALLING TRACK LIGHTING

As anyone over the age of twenty-five can tell you, indoor lighting is not your friend. If you don't believe us, just get a load of your face at the makeup counter in any large department store. Is it any wonder that you'll buy almost anything to cover up what your skin looks like when illuminated by fluorescent lights? Well, you can't control the lighting at Bloomingdale's and, besides, they have products to sell, but you can control the lighting effects in your house. Come to think of it, you're selling something, too: your own happiness. And what could make you happier than to know that, in the privacy of your own home, you look mahvelous, darling.

Joan swears that the best lighting she has ever seen is in a small restaurant on the Île St. Louis in Paris called L'Orangerie. As a matter of fact, when she recommends it to friends who are going to visit the City of Lights, she always prefaces any remarks she might make about the food by saying, "Take a look at yourself in the mirror while you're eating dinner. You'll never look better in your life!" She attributes this effect to a combination of well-placed fixtures and the use of a bulb that sends out a peach-colored glow.

Now, we're not suggesting that you can turn your home into such a lushly romantic atmosphere but, if you know what you are doing, you can create a functional and flattering lighting system that is attractive to look at, as well. Track lighting is an overhead system of lighting that, instead of relying on a single source of illumination, allows you to bathe your room in a well-balanced diffusion of light that you can use to highlight works of art and arrange to suit your own specific needs. Recessed lighting is another way of accomplishing the same objective, but we don't suggest you try to install it yourself as it relies on getting inside the wiring system of your house. With track lighting you can install the lights externally since its power source is carried along through a system of conductors which are mounted on top of the ceiling or alongside a wall. Once set up, all you have to do is plug it into the nearest outlet and magic ensues.

The Parts

A track lighting system consists of several component parts. These include:

1. The tracks
2. Couplings or connector plates
3. The track box
4. The fixture

Additional tools and materials: drill, screwdriver, mounting screws, toggle bolts, and hollow wall anchors (optional)

The tracks, themselves, come in two-, four-, and 8-foot systems. You can plug them in end to end or arrange them in any configuration you like to fit your room.

Couplings allow you to change directions with your tracks, and *connector plates* serve as the bridge between the tracks and the track box.

The track box contains the plug through which the electricity is carried.

The fixture is the direct light source to which the bulb is attached.

Installation

The first thing you will need to do is determine where you want your lighting to be. The only real restriction you have in this area is that you will need to be near a power source (a plug). If there is no power source nearby, you can run a switch-controlled power cord from the nearest receptacle to the ceiling via a special adapter you can hook into one end of your tracks. Or consider the better, safer, but more expensive option: call an electrician to have a new power source installed in the form of a ceiling box or a wall switch.

Once you have found your power source, observe your room. Which chairs or sofa do you sit in the most when you are reading, working, sewing, or watching TV, and where will you need the most light? Make a drawing of your room and seating arrangements and try playing with your lighting needs. Remember, once the fixtures are attached, you will be able to adjust them to a given area but still, they should be in the right vicinity from the get-go.

Now, and we know this will sound familiar, *turn the power off!* If there is an old ceiling fixture or chandelier already in place, disconnect it. You will eventually attach the connector directly to the ceiling box.

With a piece of chalk, lightly **mark the path** you want the tracks to follow leading out from the center of where the connector will be. **Measure the distance** carefully and put your track pieces in the same configuration on the floor directly under where they are to be installed. If everything fits and looks right, you can proceed from there. If not, make the necessary adjustments.

Holding the tracks in place, mark the places where you will need the **mounting screws**. At this point, you should follow the manufacturer's directions since the types of tracks can vary. Some fit into clips that need to be mounted separately, while others have holes that allow you to screw them directly into the ceiling.

The best way to **attach the tracks** is by locating the studs in the ceiling and drilling into them. If you can't, you will need to insert a toggle bolt or a hollow wall anchor into the hole you made before you put in any screws. When you attach the tracks, do so lightly, at first, in case there is any realignment you need to do.

Connect the leads in the track box to the wires in the ceiling box following the same instructions we gave you in the electrical chapter on how to attach a lighting fixture. Match wire to wire and, when you are set, put the plate back on the box.

Take off the cover of the track box on the face of the connecting plate, make any necessary adjustments on the tracks, and then tighten the mounting screws. *The prongs in the track plate* at the end of the track will *plug* directly into the *track box*. Put the track box back tightly when everything is in place and then twist the fixtures into place on the track in the spot you chose earlier, insert the bulbs, and turn on the power.

Once everything is in place, again sit in the spots you use the most and see if the light is to your satisfaction. If not, simply adjust the angle of the fixture.

Tip # 5: It's a Regular Work of Art

You can also run individual tracks that will shine directly on a particular object or work of art. The idea here is that the object should be highlighted and that the light should surround it, creating a similar effect to what you have seen in museums.

You might want to experiment with different strengths and colors of bulbs until you have the exact look you want.

TAKE FIVE

The idea behind these three projects was to give you a taste of what you can do with your new skills. Don't stop here, though. There are endless things you can do once you've gotten your feet wet. While there are plenty of books that can outline projects for you, we have found that it is fun to go to some of the decorator shows or to be "looky-lu's" and visit open houses in some of the better neighborhoods around town. If you see something interesting, make a sketch of it and see if you can figure out how to do it yourself. If you're stuck, take the sketch to your hardware store and get their input, buy the materials, and you're on your way.

13

Cleanliness Is Next
to Bossiness

MAKING IT ALL PERFECT

By far, the worst part of any home repair or remodeling situation is cleaning up after you are finished. But, alas, it has to be done. It's no use, after all, to build a new cabinet and then have wood shavings mark your carpet like a bad case of dandruff. Or to retouch the paint on your woodwork but leave behind dribbles of paint marking a Hansel-and-Gretel-like trail between you and your sink.

Some people are naturally neat, while others perform their tasks in a "go for broke" style which requires massive cleanup action afterwards. Jeni and Joan represent sterling examples of these polar opposites. Jeni must have just been the delight of her elementary school art teacher, whereas Joan often mistook her new blouse for an extension of her paper. Here is a case in point: Joan decided to paint the woodwork and door moldings in her den an interesting shade of gray-blue which she mixed herself. Knowing that she is a little, well, hard on her physical surroundings, she bought a drop cloth, carpet-protecting strip, and all other necessary doo-dads for trying to stay neat. Jeni walked in to find her partner's feet sticking to the drop cloth and paint trailing down her arm and onto her newly laid tile. "You're hopeless," Jeni declared, snatching the brush from her hands and *without the aid of a net or gloves,* ladies and gentlemen, proceeded to finish the job with nary a drop out of place and with a much straighter edge than Joan had been able to achieve, we might add. Joan was grateful. Pissed, but grateful.

For those of you who are like Jeni, the basic brush cleaner, Fantastik, rags and towels will probably suffice, but, for those of you who are more like Joan, you will definitely need to bring out the heavier artillery. Fortunately, there is a full fusillade of products to help. Products like Goof-Off, for example, are specifically formulated to remove latex paint from all surfaces from linoleum to carpet. The one word of caution, here, is that, not only do they stink, but the fumes are bad for you. Whenever you work with a product like Goof-Off, make sure that you leave windows open to help with the ventilation. For oil-based paint cleanups, turpentine and acetone-based products are necessary, but should be used with care. These solvents are flammable, give off toxic fumes, and are to be kept away from your skin at all costs. Don't substitute them for that expensive fruit acid peel you've always wanted—wear gloves and keep your arms and legs covered.

In general, read the ingredients and directions on the products you buy before using them. There are heavy-duty chemicals involved here, and you want to make sure that there are no possible interactions between them as well as understand what to do should they, inadvertently, come into contact with your skin or eyes. Test a small area of your carpet or other material surface first to verify color fastness. Also, make sure that you keep any cleanup product out of the reach of children and in a safe, secure, and dry place. Do not store products under the kitchen sink as many products don't do well near water. The safest idea is to store all chemical products on a high shelf in a closet or garage, away from water, gas-driven appliances whose pilots might ignite stray fumes, and the prying hands of little kiddies.

THE BASICS YOU WILL NEED

Brush cleaner
Turpentine
Goof-Off
An all-purpose cleaner like Fantastik or 409
Sponges
Rags
Paper towels
Utility knife
Bucket
Plastic bags for scraps, shavings, and other debris
*Plastic gloves for your hands (don't touch brushes or rags soaked in
   chemicals with your bare hands)*

Some people are good at cleaning up as they go along, while others prefer to wait until they are all finished. That choice is yours. Men usually do the latter, but when they are watching you, they tend to make note of your sloppiness along the way. Joan once dated a man who, literally, followed her around the kitchen with a sponge, cleaning up as she did her cooking. God forbid she lifted the lid on a soup pan to check on it— he'd be right behind her, mopping up the condensation from the lid. It was SO annoying.

TAKE FIVE

We guess, in general, you could say that good work habits do go hand in hand with how you feel about the job you are doing. Also, it is easier to gauge your progress if you are working in a clean and neat environment rather than with lots of things scattered around you.

On the other hand, if, by the time you've finished cleaning and mopping up, you are still not satisfied with the way things look, there is one more piece of equipment that could come in handy: the Yellow Pages. Just lift it out of its hiding place and open to the sections on *Cleaning* or *Janitorial Services* and let the pros handle it. We know, we know . . . that's cheating. Well, frankly, by the time you've done all this work to fix up and improve your living space, you deserve a break. Let someone else do the dirty work and get a massage instead.

14

Cocktails, Anyone?

THE LAST ROUNDUP

So, ladies, you've just survived your first foray into home repair. Was it good for you, too? Uh huh, we can tell it was from that contented smile on your face and the musky aroma of WD 40 that lingers around your hair.

You've really earned your stripes. You've plunged, you've wired, you've sawed, you've spackled, you've wrenched. But, the big question is . . . Are you a pro? We mean, how do you know you're *really* ready to tackle anything, anywhere, anyhow, anytime?

Well, just light up a cigarette, put on some soft mood music, and relax. Here's the test:

YOU KNOW YOU'RE THE FIX-IT QUEEN WHEN

The guys at Sears know you by your first name.

You carry drill bits around in your purse.

The first thing you notice about your friend's new house is that her wall nails are out of alignment.

Your husband calls YOU when the toilet starts to overflow.

A screwdriver does *not* automatically make you think of a vodka and orange juice.

You risk running your brand-new $25 Donna Karan panty hose by stooping to tighten a bolt under the sink.

You'd rather go to the tool sale at Home Depot than the January white sale at Bloomingdale's.

When your husband asks if you want a screw, you ask, "Phillips or flat head?"

You actually look forward to spring paint-up, fix-up, patch-up time.

You set your VCR to record anything dealing with tools.

Your fingers start to itch with anticipation at the thought of handling a power tool.

You get jealous whenever you see anyone wearing overalls with huge grease stains.

While you and your significant other are making love, you give him tips on how to improve his leverage.

You can't remember the last time you saw your nails extend beyond your fingertips.

You are starting to wonder how hard it would be to change the oil in your car by yourself.

All the doorknobs in your house look like last year's models.

You keep a can of turpentine in your medicine chest, right next to the moisturizing hand cream.

Your husband finds you sleepwalking to change a circuit breaker.

You know what size screw to use in your anchor . . . on sight.

You keep spare tools in the bun in your hair.

You pity any woman who doesn't know what a nail set is.

For Christmas, you want Santa to bring you a big power drill.

You love the smell of turpentine in the morning.

A vibrator looks just like a giant Tinkertoy to you now.

Your kids bring you to school for show and tell as "my mom, the repairman."

You can't remember the last time you had a repairman in your house . . . to do any repairs, that is.

You can use the words "ball cock" in a sentence without blushing.

You're proud of your calluses.

When you and your friends discuss "How big it was," you're not referring to what you used to refer to.

You keep an autographed picture of Bob Vila by your bedside.

You hang out at the local hardware store, just to "talk shop."

You no longer view your house as the enemy . . . you are master of your own universe.

About the Authors

Jeni E. Munn is an independent producer and writer. Before heading to Hollywood, she spent seven years in England, studying biology and mathematics, and wound up working in a cancer research lab at Memorial Sloan Kettering Cancer Center in New York City. Simultaneously, she fed her muse working off-off Broadway as a fund-raiser and stage manager.

In 1986, she heeded the call of the West and her future ex-husband, and moved to Los Angeles where she entered the glamorous world of show business by answering phones and picking up dry cleaning for a "very successful producer" (his words, not hers). Ultimately, she became Senior Vice President of Production for the Badham/Cohen Group at Universal Studios.

Joan Sittenfield is a television writer and producer. She started her life in show business as an actress and a dancer, then, after getting her master's degree in theater from USC, she spent her mid-twenties as a guest artist in residence, teaching acting and movement at various universities around the United States. Returning to Los Angeles, she became an independent casting director, casting television series such as *Taxi* and *The Jeffersons,* and working on the films *Once Upon a Time in America, Oh God II,* and *Bad Medicine.* For nine years she was Senior Vice President of Talent and Casting at Universal Television, where she oversaw the casting and developed the talent for over twenty shows and one hundred pilots, including *Northern Exposure, Law and Order, Coach,* and *A Year in the Life.*

For the past three years, she has had her own production company, along with Jeni Munn, developing and producing movies for television. On her own, she has written several original stories for TV movies as well as a novel and a script, both of which have been optioned for production.

Both authors live in Los Angeles.

Discard

DEMCO